THE CRYSTAL TREE

THE CRYSTAL TREE

A Structured Approach to Reading Crystals and Colored Stones

Kelynda

Whitford Press

1469 Morstein Road
West Chester, Pennsylvania 19380 USA

The Crystal Tree
by Kelynda

Library of Congress Catalog Card Number: 87-62097
International Standard Book Number: 0-914918-73-7

Edited by Julie Lockhart
192 pages
Cover design by Bob Boeberitz

Published by Whitford Press, a division of
Schiffer Publishing, Ltd.

This book may be purchased from the publisher.
Please include $2.00 postage.
Try your bookstore first.
Please send for free catalog to:
Whitford Press
c/o Schiffer Publishing, Ltd.
1469 Morstein Road
West Chester, Pennsylvania 19380

Manufactured in the United States of America.

Contents

Acknowledgments

No book is written alone, especially not a book using elements of ancient philosophies. *The Crystal Tree* owes much to the thought of the anonymous people, long dead, who first discovered the principles of astrology and numerology, who first coded the progress of the soul in the major arcana of the tarot, who first held quartz crystals to the light and sensed their power. Mystics of many persuasions have contributed to my work as well. In different ways, so have the makers of my computer and software, the people who do the actual production work of printing and binding and proofreading, and the suppliers of stones.

In practical terms, though, I must thank those directly involved. My husband Bill, who talked me into writing this book, did everything in his power to help me while I wrote it — from taking over some of my household chores to listening to my rejoicings and my laments as the book went well or badly. He is always my inspiration and my support. My mother's encouragement began when I first decided to be a writer (at about the age of five) and has been steady ever since. I treasure her advice: "You can do anything you want. Just don't wait until you're forty to find that out." Julie Lockhart, my editor, has been unfailingly enthusiastic and helpful throughout the long process of writing and production. Peter Schiffer, my publisher, took a chance on me — and I thank him.

Finally, I thank you, the reader, for listening and learning. I hope you will let me know how some of your readings turn out.

For Bill — forever

Part One

An Introduction to The Crystal Tree

1

An Introduction

In the curving paths of planets and electrons there is order; in the dark turns of all mazes there is evidence of the creating hand. The Universe reflects the thoughts of the creator. Though stars and symbols are full of meaning, colored stones may seem difficult to read. But stones are older than the constellations (though younger than the stars) and infinitely older than even the beloved symbols of the tarot. The stones predate us, and they may show us ourselves more clearly because they are so old.

On a recent trip to the Museum of Natural History in New York, I saw the fifteen-thousand-year-old remains of the knives and homes and paintings of our ice-age ancestors. I saw a section of a tree that had begun to grow fifty years or so before King Arthur was born and that was cut when my great-grandmother was a year old. And I saw the skeletons of animals from dinosaurs to common field mice. Yet nothing moved me so much as the stones: chunks of rock fluorescing in black light, crystals breaking from their matrices, precious stones left casually in the rock or set in gold as bevelled and faceted jewels, jade smoothed into delicately curved sculptures, the pillar of malachite and azurite — green swirled with blue — that looks like a squared sculpture of the earth as seen from space.

Stones endure, and they appeal to us. Their many forms and uses — a diamond in an engagement ring or a stone farmhouse's utilitarian beauty — evoke a wide range of emotions in us. In *The Crystal Tree* I have codified some of these symbolic values and made them available to you.

An important phrase here is "symbolic value." The stones are symbols for forces far beyond them, metaphors for universal concepts that are difficult to express in words. They are not the true source of the power they contain, nor are they the only expression of that power. For simplicity's sake, I use the phraseology of possession — this stone has this energy or that power — when in actuality the stone is a symbol of that energy.

Symbols serve to make us aware of what is already there, around us and in us. Amethyst, for example, influences your relations with others; however, this does not mean that carrying an amethyst will change your love life or make your friends loyal. The stone symbolizes the way you deal with people — amethyst suggests a balance of self-control and self-expression — but it is *the way you deal with people* that has the power, not the amethyst. The stone merely responds to what is already there. More specifically, you choose the amethyst because its vibration is the same as the vibration of your friendships. Carrying an amethyst can remind you of the qualities it represents; it can help you strive for those qualities by reminding you of them; however, it cannot "give" you anything.

Don't confuse shadow with substance. A wedding ring is the symbol of a marriage, but the loss of the ring doesn't end the marriage. Wearing it may remind you of the special glint of your spouse's eye or the way you felt when you first kissed; it also can remind you of the argument you had the day before yesterday. It is the marriage that has the power, not the ring.

The stones are used as mirrors to look inside yourself, to see what you already know in your deepest self but cannot discover consciously. *The Crystal Tree* does not involve calling upon exterior forces, demons, or the dead; you simply sense each stone's vibration, then use it to gain insight into yourself. As such, it is a mystical process, but not a magical one. This book is a guide to what you may find inside yourself and to the broad universal meanings symbolized by stones and Tree of Life. As you grow more adept, the interpretations given can be expanded by your insights. It is said that if you once learn to read (in the divinatory sense), you can read anything, from the flight of birds to the patterns of cracks in a city sidewalk. This is true because once you become accustomed to being in touch with your inner self — the source of your insight and your connection with the spiritual world — you can use any object to center your concentration and help you get inside yourself. With *The Crystal Tree* you use gemstones and the Kabbalistic Tree of Life. They offer a good place to start because they have certain qualities that make them more easily used and more reliable than sheep's entrails or the pattern of mushrooms in an oak forest.

The Stones of The Crystal Tree

Most of the stones included with *The Crystal Tree* are varieties of quartz: crystalline, colored, cryptocrystalline. These include the familiar and expensive crystals, amethysts, and rose quartzes, but also jaspers, agates, and onyx, all of which are quartz-based rocks. In some ways, the choice is not surprising: fully 95 percent of the earth's crust is made up of silicon dioxide,[1] and quartz is silicon dioxide. Over time, silicon dioxide grows into the six-sided, light-refracting quartz crystal. (For the sake of simplicity, we will refer to quartz crystals simply as crystals, though there are many other kinds of crystals.) Sometimes the silicon dioxide is tinged with another mineral, which gives it a color. Depending on the mineral, the crystalline quartz can become grey, purple, yellow, pink — almost any color.

Silicon dioxide is as common as sand. In fact, most sand is silicon dioxide. So is most window glass. What qualities does this very ordinary mineral have that make it suitable for divination?

Shouldn't only the rarest and most precious things be used for meditation?

The very commonness of silicon dioxide is a point in its favor. There is an elitist idea that 95 percent of everything is garbage (usually it's not phrased so politely); silicon dioxide turns that idea on its head. Depending on how it is used and what structures it takes on, silicon dioxide can be the most practical or the most precious of stones. In all its forms, it expresses one or more of its three essential qualities: intelligence, intuition, and communication.

Intelligence

Intelligence is both receptive and retentive. We usually honor the retentiveness (memory), but tend to give short shrift to receptiveness (perception). Because everyone's perception is filtered through their own experience, it is sometimes hard to communicate one's unique vision. Moreover, it is easy to for others to deny or downplay perceptions that are inconvenient or embarrassing to them by saying that such perceptions are biased or inaccurate — as they sometimes are. Thus we have come to rely far more on memory and on standardized images of behavior than on genuine perception.

The intelligence of silicon dioxide is shown both as memory and as perception. How can sand remember? Make it into a computer chip. Silicon Valley, the California high-tech area, is named for the computer chips — and the substance — that made it possible. These words were written with the help of a computer: silicon dioxide spreading its own fame. Quartz watches and clocks also remember the complexities of the calendar and the rhythm of the Universe with their steady pulsing. Silicon dioxide, as optical quartz, is perceptive in a very concrete way: It is ground into lenses for microscopes and telescopes, which enable us to see inward and outward. Even eyeglass lenses are made of silicon dioxide, though no glass made has the optical qualities of crystalline quartz.

Intuition

Intuition knows, but not in a rational sense; its information comes from the personal unconscious and the collective unconscious,[2] and also embraces the functions of imagination and creation. For instance, silicon dioxide *knows* where gold is and goes there;[3] we can trace gold deposits by following quartz veins. In the shape of crystal balls, quartz is used for meditation and the seeking of visions. The colored stones of *The Crystal Tree* work on the same principle of the intuitive power of quartz.[4]

Communication

How can silicon dioxide communicate? Crystals were used in early radio sets. Fiber optic lines have begun to carry telephone conversations and computer messages, and fiber optic lines are made of glass: silicon dioxide. For centuries, glass, in the form of stained-glass windows, has been one of the greatest expressions of our love for God, a communication both to God and to those who see it, even centuries after its intricate designs were made.

Why Can You Tell Fortunes with Crystals?

Although you agree that silicon dioxide has many diverse uses, you still may not be convinced that crystals are useful in divination. You still may be of the attitude that only rare and expensive materials are suitable carriers of symbolism: diamonds have meaning, pebbles have none. This attitude is wrong on several counts. First, it presupposes that worldly value has anything to do with spiritual value. Second, it assumes that the rare is more important than the common. Third, it overlooks the special qualities of silicon dioxide discussed above.

Any divination requires three qualities: intelligence, intuition, and communication. Intelligence perceives rationally — it actually sees the stones laid out and understands their pattern — and remembers. Intuition provides the psychic flow and creates the symbols that will be most meaningful to the questioner. Communication between reader and questioner, or between the developer of a system and its user, provides a key to the interpretation and a way of discussing it. Silicon dioxide in whatever form is obviously useful for divination, because it is already linked with these three qualities.

Some forms of silicon dioxide are easier to use than others; though you can read sand or sandstone, it's more convenient to work with small pieces of stone. Quartz's optical qualities aid concentration by focusing the light and intensifying the psychic flow. (Quartz does not create either the light or the psychic flow, however.) Colored stones are particularly useful in divination since each color and form has its own vibration and meaning. The beauty of their colors stimulates the psychic flow, even in people who are not full-fledged mystics. The classic crystal ball is both useful and beautiful, but it takes training and discipline to use it properly; it is a tool for those who are already psychically aware. It evokes visions for those who are already open to them, but it offers little insight to the uninitiated.

Who Can Use The Crystal Tree?

The Crystal Tree is designed so that anyone can use it. It will work for those of you who have never held a tarot card in your hand or looked up your own sun sign, and it will work for expert astrologers and tarot readers who have been doing mystical and psychic work all their lives. (The connections between *The Crystal Tree* and other psychic arts are explored in chapters 6, 7, and 8).

The Crystal Tree provides interpretations on at least three levels. The physical level deals with events, ordinary actions, and ideas. The psychological level relates to underlying motives, character traits, and emotional problems. The spiritual level is associated with the Way of Heaven, your progress on the Path (your individual spiritual quest), and your relations with the Inner Light. All three levels can be present in any reading. There is also another factor in any reading, which is called the Shadow. The Shadow is your dark, hidden side and the dark side of each stone's meanings.

Each of the eighteen stones has its own set of meanings (see chapter 2). Here they are combined with the meanings of the Tree of Life. The Tree of Life, an ancient symbol from the Jewish Kabbala, is a model of the spiritual quest (described and interpreted in chapter 4). Its ten *sephiroth* (singular, *sephirah*) each deal with a different step along the path or part of life. All basic meanings and the instructions for use are summarized in Appendix A; fuller interpretations are found in the text.

To use *The Crystal Tree* to your best advantage, read the chapters on the Tree of Life and the stones before you try to do a reading. You should look at the diagram of the Tree of Life as you study the text; when you read about the stones, you should examine each in turn. (It helps tremendously if you hold them as you read; as I wrote each section, the stone I was describing was there before me, and I held and rubbed it while I thought about the next sentence.)

Later, you may want to go back and read Part Four, which covers the links with other psychic arts. When you are thoroughly familiar with *The Crystal Tree*, Part Five will tell you how to expand it to suit your needs.

Notes

1. D. G. A. Whitten and J. V. R. Brooks, *The Penguin Dictionary of Geology* (London: Penguin, 1972), p. 413.

2. Throughout the book, I use "unconscious" instead of "subconscious" to avoid confusion. The subconscious is a Freudian concept — to oversimplify, a place that is full of complexes and repressions. The Jungian unconscious — including the collective unconscious — is not only a place where painful memories are stored, but also a place of rich creativity and nourishment. The concepts are essentially different. For more information, see C. G. Jung, *Analytical Psychology: Its Theory and Practice* (New York: Vintage, 1970). The basic viewpoint of this book is Jungian, and Jungian terms and concepts will be used throughout.

3. John McPhee, *Basin and Range* (New York: Farrar, Straus, and Giroux, 1981), pp. 32, 33.

4. The intuitive and creative aspects of silicon dioxide construct much of our daily lives. The tangible expression of its creative vision is most familiar in sand and sandstone. Sand is used in the concrete of buildings, sidewalks, and streets; sandstone shapes not only individual stone buildings, from barns to castles, but also shapes the land it lies under. (A geologist or photo interpreter can look at a topographic map or an aerial photograph and tell which rocks underlie the area; each has a distinctive morphology, known as a landform. See Arthur L. Bloom, *Geomorphology: A Systematic Analysis of Late Cenozoic Landforms* (Englewood Cliffs, NJ: Prentice-Hall, 1978), p. 9. Even in the form of glass, silicon dioxide shapes and allows light into our buildings; we eat from glass dishes and drink from containers called glasses.

Part Two

What Is The Crystal Tree?

2

The Stones

The eighteen stones of *The Crystal Tree* were chosen to form a whole: a spectrum of color and meaning. Most are assigned to a specific sephirah (branch of the Tree of Life) where they find their fullest expression, just as a planet finds its fullest expression in the astrological sign it rules.

Each stone in *The Crystal Tree* has meaning on a number of different levels. The first is the physical plane, where we live ordinary life and where the stones predict events or explain actions. The second is the psychological plane, where motives and karma come up. The third level is the spiritual plane, where our progress on the Path — whatever path we take — is measured and explained. The Shadow, the dark side of any quality, haunts all three planes. People are said to have the faults of their virtues: this is what is meant by the Shadow.

A key to identifying the different gemstones follows. The interpretations of the stones have been arranged according to the sephirah to which each belongs. Six stones — the clear, grey, and black stones — belong to no particular sephirah but are equally at home in each; they are listed last.

Following the key to identifying the stones are two sections to help you interpret their meanings. The first of these sections is a brief encapsulization; the second deals with each stone's meanings in greater depth. The interpretations express the qualities of the person who has chosen the stone or the person about/for whom the reading is done. The stones symbolize or express certain qualities; they do not bestow them.

How to Identify the Stones

Red

> **Rose quartz:** translucent, pale pink
> **Red cullet:** transparent, blood red

Orange

> **Jasper:** opaque, dark orange, fine-grained
> **Carnelian:** semi-opaque, orange, no grain, often banded

Brown/Yellow

> **Cat's-eye:** opaque, yellowish brown, shines like satin
> **Brown agate:** translucent brown, sometimes banded with white

Green

> **Green quartz:** opaque, mottled pale green
> **Aventurine:** opaque, shiny dark green

Blue/Grey

> **Hematite:** opaque, metallic steely gray
> **Sodalite:** opaque, very dark blue

Purple

> **Chevron amethyst:** translucent, purple banded with clear or white
> **Amethyst:** translucent, rich purple

White/Clear

    Crystal (clear): clear as glass
    Crystal (half-clear): cloudy
    Silent stone: opaque, white

Black/Grey

    Montana agate: cloudy, translucent, with dark flecks
    Smoky quartz: dark grey, translucent when held to light
    Onyx: opaque, black, shiny

A Brief Interpretation of the Stones

Rose Quartz
Sephirah: Crown

    Physical: Friendship, intimacy, closeness.
    Psychological: Harmony and affection; close family ties; the need for love and approval.
    Spiritual: Surrender to God.
    Shadow: Giving in, lack of self-assertion, going along with the crowd.

Red Cullet
Sephirah: Crown

    Physical: Individualism, passion, and sexuality.
    Psychological: Passion, creation, art. Independence and rebellion.
    Spiritual: Spiritual transformation and renewal, the spirit of seeking.
    Shadow: Jealousy, self-centeredness.

Jasper
Sephirah: Wisdom

    Physical: Restlessness, change, curiosity.

Psychological: Spirit of seeking, self-examination, analysis.

Spiritual: The spirit of the quest, of the pilgrim.

Shadow: Change for its own sake — or the refusal to change and grow.

Carnelian
Sephirah: Understanding

Physical: Warm and affectionate friendships, parties, and celebrations.

Psychological: Emotional ties based on knowledge of the other person, not on mystery and uncertainty. The need to understand and analyze relationships.

Spiritual: Reverence for life. The attitude that pleasure is of God and is therefore holy. Mystical union with God and all creation.

Shadow: Manipulativeness, lack of self-respect, overindulgence, hiding behind a social group.

Cat's-Eye
Sephirah: Mercy

Physical: Insight, shrewdness, vision.

Psychological: The gift of understanding others' problems. Often the mark of someone who is dedicated to helping others.

Spiritual: Willingness to forgive, understanding the flaws of yourself and others.

Shadow: Judgmental spirit, cattiness, gossip.

Brown Agate
Sephirah: Severity

Physical: Caution and good judgment. Slow and careful preparation.

Psychological: Self-discipline.

Spiritual: Penance, justice, scrupulous fairness.

Shadow: Pessimism, gloom, worry, often over petty matters. Insecurity and fear.

Green Quartz
Sephirah: Beauty

Physical: Strength of character, self-esteem.

Psychological: Blending the unconscious with the conscious. Willingness to face your own dark side. The ability to interpret dreams.

Spiritual: The Kingdom of God within you.

Shadow: Nightmares, phobias, emotional problems. The separation of spiritual and physical life.

Aventurine
Sephirah: Beauty

Physical: Great physical enjoyment, health, taking pleasure in the body.

Psychological: Balance between body, soul, and spirit. A healthy and innocent enjoyment of physical pleasures.

Spiritual: Freely offering of the body to God.

Shadow: Physical illness, stress, and separation from (or too much absorption in) the body.

Hematite
Sephirah: Victory

Physical: Enduring love, desire controlled by idealism, complete commitment.

Psychological: The discipline to transform dreams into reality. Sustained commitment to a dream.

Spiritual: Continuing devotion to God despite adverse circumstances.

Shadow: Rigidity, fault-finding. Inability to make a commitment or stick to a project.

Sodalite
Sephirah: Splendor

Physical: Achievement, success, hard work rewarded.

Psychological: Getting your just deserts — knowing what you deserve and asking for it.
Spiritual: Freedom from greed, taking no thought for the morrow.
Shadow: Materialism, greed, lack of compassion.

Chevron Amethyst
Sephirah: Foundation

Physical: Organization, structure, neatness.
Psychological: The final integration of the personality.
Spiritual: The order of heaven.
Shadow: Snobbishness, wrong priorities, inhuman bureaucracy.

Amethyst
Sephirah: Kingdom

Physical: Psychic talents combined with common sense. Great success.
Psychological: Psychic powers used well, self-knowledge and self-control.
Spiritual: A true spirit. Proper values.
Shadow: Using psychic knowledge for destructive purposes (very dangerous).

Crystal (clear)

Physical: Psychic abilities and clarity of outlook. Emotional harmony and peace.
Psychological: The integrated personality. Good relationships with others based on self-respect.
Spiritual: Clear views of spiritual truth.
Shadow: Arrogance, fear of change.

Crystal (half-clear)

Physical: Confusion, hasty or prejudiced thinking. Not letting yourself see the whole situation.

Psychological: Hiding the truth from yourself (usually to protect someone else).

Spiritual: The beginning of wisdom: knowing that you don't know.

Shadow: Refusing to trust yourself.

Silent stone (white)

Physical: New beginnings and ideas.

Psychological: Waiting for the right time to make new beginnings.

Spiritual: The start of a new way of thinking. Protecting new ideas from hostile people.

Shadow: Overcaution or overeagerness.

Montana Agate

Physical: Memories and persons from the past turn up. Opportunities to correct past mistakes.

Psychological: Unconscious worries or influences from the past.

Spiritual: Remembering past problems in order to avoid them in the future.

Shadow: Restraint, fear, lack of forgiveness of yourself and others.

Smoky Quartz

Physical: The ability or need to conceal yourself from other people. A dramatic temperament.

Psychological: Hiding your true self in order to be liked or accepted. Adaptability.

Spiritual: Struggling to find a true path. The faith is there, but the way is not evident.

Shadow: Self-blame, oversensitiveness.

Onyx

Physical: Strength, courage, endurance.

Psychological: Getting to the root of the problem — a painful but necessary process.

Spiritual: Rebirth after a period of suffering and dryness.

Shadow: Giving up; refusing to enjoy anything for fear it will be taken away.

More Complete Interpretations of the Stones

Rose Quartz
Sephirah: Crown

Rose quartz has the spiritual strength to be gentle. Like all the quartzes, it is perceptive and intellectual, but it is not as fiery as the other quartzes. On all three levels — physical, psychological, and spiritual — it represents the meek who will inherit the earth. Meekness is not weakness; "meek" is translated in the New American Standard Bible as "gentle."[1] Nor is it a negative quality — a lack of spirit — but a positive one: the presence of Spirit enough to keep rose quartz calm and balanced. The gentle are at ease with themselves and the world, so they have no need to create fusses, insist on their own importance, or bluster and brag.

So far, rose quartz sounds like the Victorian heroines (Little Eva in Uncle Tom's Cabin, Beth in Little Women), quiet saints who die young. But there is more force to rose quartz than that. Gentleness is revealed in the laid-back lifestyle called for by the experts who champion Type B personalities and biofeedback. We are so used to measuring "health" (mental and physical) by aggressiveness that we dismiss gentler qualities as colorless and weak, if not neurotic.

Moreover, there is a potent force at work here: the force of ease. In general, we invite our own troubles, at least the minor worries that cause so much daily stress and can result in illness. By keeping your priorities in focus and appreciating the holiness of daily life, you can refuse to participate in the rat race. A gentle, easygoing attitude can accomplish more than all the frenzied scurrying of Wall Street.

Red cullet
Sephirah: Crown

On a physical level, red cullet is dramatic, passionate, highly individual — and a little false sometimes. Its desire for first place can make it jealous of others' worth and callous to their pain; red cullet has been known to do almost anything to get attention. Red cullet is sometimes rebellious not out of a desire to see genuine change but for kicks — the excitement of being important, the chance to shine others down. Its intense sexuality is rooted less in exuberant enjoyment than in a need to prove itself desirable and in taking pleasure from shocking less flamboyant characters. In other words, red cullet likes to create scenes, dramatize itself, make itself important, because it (alone of the stones in *The Crystal Tree*) is an artificial stone. It's composed of the same silicon dioxide that naturally makes up quartz crystals, with added minerals for color, but it is a created stone.

The spirit of self-transformation supplies the psychological and spiritual dimensions of red cullet. To a certain extent, we all create ourselves: by our choice of friends and clothes, by what we emphasize and suppress in our personalities, by what tastes and opinions we acquire and discard. We look for role models and (especially as teenagers) try out different looks, personalities, ways of speaking. Self-creation is natural and probably necessary; by it we learn which traits are truly our own and which are merely grafted on to us by parents, teachers, and peers. The process, however, is designed to help us find our real selves — the clothes, opinions, friends, tastes that truly express us — and it can go awry when it is used to create a false self that merely conforms to expectations or peer pressure. Some people, though, have learned to hate or fear their true selves. They may be unwilling or unable to go through the painful process of self-healing, so instead they create a persona: a false and usually dramatic image. The insecure man who brags about his imagined exploits in love, war, and business is an example of the negative side of self-creation and of red cullet.

On the positive side, the created persona or the self discovered through the energies of red cullet can be remarkably strong. Red cullet symbolizes writers who create characters from the depths of their own self-knowledge. It inspires any artist who transcends his or her own self by expressing that self in music, painting, dance, sculpture. Red cullet's energy is lent to all who succeed at changing their lives: by getting an education when this is not traditional in their families, by fighting an addiction, by healing themselves through psychotherapy, by struggling to conquer physical illness or injury or handicap.

On a spiritual level, red cullet symbolizes a transformed life, a life that is given over to God. Here red cullet's refining fire burns away the worldly and destructive and inspires the spiritual. Saint Francis of Assisi, who was a wealthy and somewhat vain young man, was transformed by prayer into a loving, giving person who tried to heap his ever-increasing love on other people and animals. His conversion burned away the worldly — ambition, vanity, pride — and substituted an all-embracing passion for life and a great wonder at the beauty of the created world. Eight hundred years later, his love and influence are still felt.[2] Transformations take place every day, in minor ways as well as major, when the meretricious is seen in all its falsity and the glories of heaven become manifest.

Red Jasper
Sephirah: Wisdom

Jasper comes in many forms and guises. Red jasper, a fine-grained, dark orange stone, is the jasper of Wisdom.

Red jasper indicates a restless, seeking nature that may express itself as a perpetual desire for change. At its worst, it can symbolize the person who is unable to hold a job, handle a love affair, or put down roots for more than a few weeks or months. Conversely, some people are so terrified of their strong jasper connections that they clamp down on any kind of change at all, terrified that one change would start a landslide of inescapable and unstoppable transformation.

The questing spirit can show itself in positive ways. On a purely physical level, red jasper indicates intelligence, curiosity, and drive. It can produce gossips, but it also inspires scientists, detectives, psychologists, reporters, and insatiable readers. Red jasper looks always for the why of things; it loves to learn. Psychologically, red jasper relates to the spirit of self-analysis, which is the willingness to look for the root causes of emotional traumas.

It is spiritually, though, that red jasper has its finest moments. The restless, seeking nature that turns to God does so with a pained, passionate, endless desire. John Donne is perhaps the best example of this energy. He was a handsome poet whose explicit love lyrics are still extraordinarily powerful. His passions wrecked his career and landed him in prison. He became a prominent churchman, considered by some to be the finest preacher since Saint Paul, whose exquisitely phrased poetry is passionate for but never sure of God. Most people know him as the author of the *Devotions*: "Ask not for whom the bell tolls, it tolls for thee."[3] Through all of Donne's poetry and prose, from his amorous lyrics to his great sermons, runs the spirit of questing; he is never self-satisfied but eager to enjoy the moment, desiring unnameable things and exerting full strength to find them. This is the power of red jasper. Its searching spirit and great energy are bound to find something.

Carnelian
Sephirah: Understanding

Carnelian's color expresses the warm and affectionate nature of this stone's energy. Like a popular person, carnelian is lively, warm-hearted, cheerful, and easygoing. However, it can become manipulative, secretly despising the people it charms, or it can serve as a mask to hide deeper problems. Overindulgence, in any of its many forms, also can be a problem; carnelian is so carefree that it can be careless — with money, with drugs or alcohol, with food, with its own time.

Physically, carnelian denotes parties, friendships, enjoyment. Psychologically, it goes deeper: the friendships and other relationships are solidly based on the partners' understanding one another. Conversation is the key to carnelian's energy here; mere blood ties or business connections are not enough to develop the relationships governed by carnelian. Talking about thoughts, emotions, and experiences is necessary. Sometimes, however, the talking can take over the relationship, and the need to understand and analyze becomes obsessive.

On a spiritual level, carnelian achieves a mystical union with God and the created Universe through its sense of the glory of all created things and the sweetness of God's love. It is not stern and ascetic; it enjoys the wealth of innocent pleasures provided for our refreshment. To carnelian, all life is holy and beautiful; it enjoys the pleasures and the fun of everyday actions and events. Carnelian's holiness is like that of a little child, watching the world with new eyes, forgiving easily, and in the midst of sorrows finding comfort and love in the natural world.

Cat's-Eye
Sephirah: Mercy

Cat's-eye often seems dark when you first pick it up, but turn it in your hands and it catches the light with a golden sheen. It looks always for the best; it can be watchful, shrewd, insightful, understanding, and forgiving, depending on what "best" it is looking for. When the best is bad, it can cause a great deal of damage through gossip, pessimism, inducing guilt in others, and constant criticism.

On the physical level, cat's-eye can watch for personal advantage, the most practical way of doing a job and new ways of making money. It's hard to fool cat's-eye; because it pays attention and watches for details, it knows much that is usually missed.

On a psychological level, cat's-eye sees others' problems and notes connections between apparently unrelated events. It is often the mark of someone dedicated to helping others: a psychotherapist, a doctor or nurse, a pastor, a mother, a psychic counselor. All these professions require keen observation of physical, emotional, or psychic problems. However, there are many people who don't pursue any of these fields professionally who are also strongly imbued with cat's-eye talents.

On a spiritual level, cat's-eye sees sins and faults, and it forgives. Its vision is wide enough to include God's mercy and forgiveness as well as sin and wrong. Not only can cat's-eye forgive the sins of others, but also those of the self — usually the hardest to forgive.

Brown Agate
Sephirah: Severity

Brown agate lacks the brilliant shine of cat's-eye and the bright coloration of the other stones. Its dark brown surface hardly shows its translucence, though many specimens are translucent.

It seems the opposite of cat's-eye, for brown agate looks not for the best but for possible problems and difficulties. Yet it also denotes common sense, practicality, good judgment. However, it can lapse into pessimism, worry (often over petty matters), and insecurity; some people take this quality so far that they can no longer enjoy anything but disasters, suspicion, and gloom. They love to complain; they foresee major catastrophes (the world going to the dogs) but never put out a hand to stop it. Their own personal problems are never dealt with, perhaps because they are too cautious to change anything in their lives. They seem to fear happiness and enjoy worry.

Brown agate in its positive, physical aspect sees ahead to troubles and prepares for them; it doesn't panic or become flustered. It is generally calm, strong, disciplined; though unglamorous, it is necessary and useful — two of the qualities it most values. Brown agate is well organized, competent, and hardworking. Perhaps brown agate can be valued best by those who have had to suffer under improvident parents, impractical bosses, or irresponsible roommates and spouses. Then the unassuming qualities of foresight and responsibility take on new luster.

On a psychological level, brown agate represents self-discipline: the willingness to work hard and, if necessary, suffer a little now in order to reap good results later. Brown agate takes responsibility for itself; it doesn't wait for someone else to heal its wounds, but learns to tend them itself, then uses its experience to help others.

On a spiritual level, brown agate pursues justice and fairness. Sometimes it does penance or tries to make up for its sins; it also willingly undergoes times of self-deprivation, as in the Lenten fasts, because such things teach what is truly necessary and what superfluous. The cleansing effect of fasts is a manifestation of the energy symbolized by brown agate.

Green Quartz
Sephirah: Beauty

Just as the Tree of Life itself does, green quartz represents a reconciliation of opposites. It reconciles the pleasures and exuberance of created life with the pure intellectual and spiritual vibrations of crystal. Badly manifested, it can result in nightmares and phobias — fears that are not consciously dealt with turning up in unconscious and painful ways. It can show a sense of imprisonment, the lonely spirit warring with the hostile body, and several kinds of health problems. Green quartz imbalances often cause people to live in a compartmentalized way, with parts of their lives hidden and shut off from the others.

In a physical sense, green quartz represents self-respect based on inner balance. When all parts of the self are acknowledged and honored, the whole person is strong. "A house divided against itself will not stand";[4] neither will a person. The strength of character it creates is not a gritted-teeth, stoic willpower but a fundamental wholeness.

On a psychological level, this strength of character is developed by facing and accepting your own unconscious and learning to draw on its strengths instead of repressing it. This can be expressed by a willingness to remember and interpret your own dreams: the unconscious speaking to the conscious as directly as it can.

On a spiritual level, green quartz indicates reconciliation between your will and God's. "The Kingdom of God is within you": all that light, all that joy, is available now.[5] It isn't something that will come someday but a way to live every day. This mystical doctrine cannot be explained, but it can be experienced by faith. An example — and I can only speak metaphorically and by example — is living a balanced and complete life, enjoying and understanding earthly pleasures while following the way of heaven, loving and forgiving those who do wrong (including yourself) while hating the sin.

Aventurine
Sephirah: Beauty

Aventurine is related to physical health and strength, as well as a kind of astonished joy in the flesh, like young animals kicking up their heels in play. This absorption in the body can be manifested as hypochondria and vanity, or it may be denied entirely by those who have learned to hate and fear the flesh, seeing it as an occasion for sin or a storehouse of pain. Aventurine can also indicate incipient stress or physical illness.

Aventurine is so physical that its interpretation on the physical plane is its primary meaning. It offers healthy and innocent enjoyment of physical pleasures, from games and exercise to good food to lovemaking. Its natural exuberance is sometimes known as "animal spirits," and is indeed based on physical pleasures. Even an enjoyment of nature and the outdoors comes under aventurine's domain. Less intellectual than instinctual, this stone is experienced through the senses.

On a psychological level, aventurine indicates a healthy balance between body, mind, soul, and spirit. Sadly, the aventurine energies often are impaired in childhood. Though children naturally enjoy running around and playing, unpleasant experiences (for example, early, severe illness or pain; physical or sexual abuse; even over-competitive gym classes that mock less coordinated children) can cause one to retreat from the physical level.

On a spiritual level, aventurine represents offering the body to God. Though this aspect of aventurine is usually thought of as celibacy, it is more likely to be expressed as chastity: putting all sexual experiences into a spiritual framework. Chastity, though, is not the only issue here; offering the body to God includes offering all exercise, food and drink, health and illness, physical appearance and aging. In some ways, chastity is less important than your general attitude toward the body. Chastity will follow when all else is in the right place, but the destructiveness of wrong sexual behavior has been emphasized so strongly that we tend to ignore the effects of other kinds of bodily abuses.

Hematite
Sephirah: Victory

Hematite, the grey-blue ore of iron, is the only metallic stone in *The Crystal Tree*. It belongs to the sephirah Severity, the domain of love and discipline, and iron — the dominant substance in hematite — exemplifies both.

Though iron is usually thought of as a military substance, there are equally good reasons for iron to be symbolic of love. Iron is tough and durable; it tolerates wide extremes of temperature; under ordinary circumstances it holds its own shape, but it also can be heated and reshaped at will. Love too is tough and durable, tolerant of changes in outward circumstance, tenacious but willing to change when change is needed. Neither love nor iron wears out. The heart — always symbolic of love — pumps blood that, without iron, would be pale and useless; it is iron that carries the oxygen cells need.

Hematite energies are constructive, but they can be used improperly. Self-discipline may become rigid and judgmental; love's growth toward perfection may be twisted into irritable fault-finding. Some people may find hematite's discipline too frightening; they become dilettantes who avoid the pain of self-transformation by flitting from romance to romance or by refusing to commit themselves to their work.

On a physical level, hematite symbolizes the process of falling in love, making a commitment, and learning to love and live with another person. Hematite is an iron ore that needs to be refined, a process that burns away the impurities and leaves the metal. It is analogous to the changes in a relationship over time: the transformation of an attraction into a lifelong bond.

On a psychological level, hematite represents the discipline needed to transform any dream into reality. If you dream of being a writer, you need the discipline to go on writing even when there are no apparent rewards. If you dream of being an engineer, you need the discipline to study the necessary mathematics. Hematite bridges the gap between where you stand now and where you want to be, but you have to cross that bridge yourself with steady, daily work. Any dream requires discipline, and it is love — the true love of the goal — that can supply this discipline.

On a spiritual level, hematite is the discipline that keeps the seeker on the Path even when the world seems dry and dead. Instead of focusing on the emotions of weariness and despair, the seeker focuses on the duty to be done and the prayers to be said. It is simple, faithful persistence in the spiritual life despite outside events and inner fears and sorrows.[6]

Sodalite
Sephirah: Splendor

Sodalite's rich blue color — similar to the more famous and expensive lapis lazuli — is the indication of rewards at hand. Sodalite offers success and achievement, but in the process it can become greedy and materialistic. Worse, it can lose compassion for those who are less materially fortunate.

On a physical level sodalite means hard work rewarded. Raises, promotions, material comforts, praise, and increased responsibility all come under sodalite's domain. The hard work has to be present, though; sodalite honors dedication, craftsmanship, honesty, and responsibility. Half-heartedness, sloppiness, dishonesty, and irresponsibility have their own, quite different rewards.

On a psychological level, sodalite deals with realistically valuing yourself and others. This kind of judgment requires clear priorities and a certain disinterestedness; when you judge an action, your decision must not be influenced by your feelings for a person or your relationship to him or her. Even if you judge yourself more harshly than you would anyone else, you have missed the point. Being just and fair is the goal of sodalite. Often people who judge themselves with draconian harshness in some areas are blind or indulgent to other, perhaps more damaging faults. Sodalite cultivates clarity of outlook; only when this is achieved can you claim a truly just reward.

On a spiritual level, sodalite goes beyond the question of rewards and into an area of total trust in God. Taking "no thought for the morrow,"[7] it looks only to heaven for its daily support — the opposite of sodalite's shadow, which is greed. Though this level does not preclude such practical items as wills, financial planning, or a job, it makes use of them in the full knowledge that money itself is meaningless, that it is truly God who supports and feeds us, and that the whole monetary system could be swept away tomorrow.

Chevron Amethyst
Sephirah: Foundation

Chevron amethyst is a amethyst banded with pure quartz. It represents the contact between the spiritual world and the physical world. Like all crystals, chevron amethyst is innately organized and structured. Its structure, however, can be turned to negative uses; it can be snobbish, caught in byzantine complexities of bureaucratic red tape, or it can become so enmeshed in its own exquisite structure that it loses all sense of priority.

On a physical level chevron amethyst deals with organization, neatness, and structure. It wants to clear up messy details, take care of loose ends, create or mend patterns of conduct, and sometimes it forces others into its ritual red tape. Its influence on an editor, bookkeeper, or anyone else whose work is a mass of details is excellent. Chevron amethyst is also the stone of philosophy, which attempts to understand and then express (in careful, neat syllogisms) the meaning of the Universe. Chevron amethyst creates order out of chaos.

On a psychological level, chevron amethyst is the final integration of the personality: the last threshhold of balance. Though it may seem to be too static for a symbol of mental health, crystals in their self-confident rightness — each following its own proper pattern, adding new layers in an endless dance of expansion, refracting light in lovely clarity, utterly coherent — beautifully express the idea of a healthy self becoming fully alive and fully itself.

On a spiritual level, chevron amethyst crystals are a symbol of the order of heaven: the extraordinary and delicate structures of the Divine. Creation is a pattern, and the resonance of it is ideally mirrored in the crystal. The shape of a solar system echoes the shape of the atoms that make it up, illustrating the great law of correspondences: "As above, so below."

Amethyst
Sephirah: Kingdom

The amethyst traditionally protects against a lack of self-control. It is a kind of talisman of rightness; its energies teach the appropriate use of psychic powers. If the amethyst energy is overridden, psychic powers can be used for evil instead of good, and that is a destructive game indeed. When used for evil, these powers may become unreliable or be taken away altogether. And the evil wishes always rebound on the one making them.

On a physical level the amethyst signifies great success. Amethyst's energy indicates both psychic talent and common sense, which help you to sniff out dishonesty, bizarre situations, exploitive people, and psychic vampires, and avoid them. Amethyst is also a quartz crystal and as such it focuses energy. If that focused energy is directed in the right places, it can result in great achievements.

On a psychological level, amethyst represents self-knowledge and self-control. Here the focusing effect works both inwardly and outwardly. Inward, it clarifies the self's actions and thoughts and perceives the patterns behind them, distilling memory into self-knowledge; outward, it intensifies the vague desire to be strong and good into self-control.

On a spiritual level, the amethyst symbolizes a true spirit — not true in the sense of real but in the sense of honest, faithful, dependable, true as steel. When the spirit is expressed completely, through every action and thought, it is true: it has integrity. This does not mean that every passing impulse is a message from the spirit, however, or that to be true to yourself you must steal, rape, wreck, punch, gorge, and mock as your fancy prompts you. Self-control is an energy of amethyst; so is this strange and apparently contradictory virtue of integrity. How are they to be reconciled?

The spirit — the self — is born with certain inherent strengths. We are born with tendencies to certain kinds of goodness, but we are prey to certain temptations as well. Environment encourages some tendencies and not others, sometimes tragically persuading the spirit that a permanent disguise is the only way to survive at all. Becoming spiritually aware is a long process of, among other things, becoming yourself: the ideal self, the spirit's highest potential. Thus self-control is needed to curb the bent toward self-debasement. Self-debasement does not necessarily mean acts of spectacular carnage; it may mean simply doing nothing and letting apathy destroy any positive potential; it may mean perverting your talents in an unworthy work or for a wicked cause. Thus self-control and self-fulfillment — integrity — become allies in the struggle to become yourself.

Crystal (clear)

The clear crystal, traditionally used for divination, evokes visions by its purity; light passes through it to be concentrated and focused. The structure of the crystal itself acts as a lens. Misused, that serene orderliness can become arrogant and stiff; the structure can be so contented that it discourages and eventually forbids change or growth.

On a physical level the crystal indicates psychic abilities and a clear outlook. Not necessarily visionary in the sense of dreaming of great things, the crystal is clear-sighted and not easily fooled. Its structure is harmonious, so it loves peace and emotional concord; its purity demands that all things near it be pure.

On a psychological level, the crystal symbolizes the integrated personality in action, creating strong and healthy relationships with others. Truthfulness, mutual respect, and a balance of power and effort are all typical of crystal's influence. Moreover, the crystal wants to understand; it listens with deep concentration and responds from its heart.

On a spiritual level, the crystal represents the clear light of truth. It is as "wise as serpents and as innocent as doves";[8] it reflects and concentrates spiritual power. The crystal is willing to see; its extraordinary insight and spiritual strength come from the fact that it has patterned itself with that single objective in mind: to see, to make things clearer. Because of that concentration, it can start a fire with sunlight alone.

Crystal (half-clear)

The half-clear crystal is the same material and structure as the clear crystal, but it is not polished as rigorously. Therefore, its sight is muddied by circumstance. The half-clear crystal doesn't trust its own insight, relying instead on traditional prejudices or half-understood dogma. Though one of crystal's functions is to listen intently to others, the half-clear crystal listens without having the clear crystal's cool judgment, flawless logic, and knowledge of truth. It often comes to the wrong conclusions and is swayed by the last person who speaks to it.

On a physical level the half-clear crystal means confusion, deception, and hasty judgments. The half-clear crystal would often rather not know the truth because knowing would entail changing. Change in response to the will of heaven — changing to become better and to remove flaws — is the polishing process that lets the light into the clear crystal, and the half-clear crystal fears both pain and change.

On a psychological level, the half-clear crystal knows but cannot bear the truth. It lies or conceals evidence to protect someone else and to protect itself from the agony of admitting the truth. This lying is often done quite unconsciously, but the unconscious also supplies the truth (which the poor half-clear crystal cannot and will not see). Thus psychotherapists can analyze drawings, poetry, and dreams (all of which have a unconscious content) to see what things a client is unable to talk about. Because even the most shattered and distressed person is a whole (though, perhaps, unable to put all the pieces in touch with one another), everything a person does or creates reflects the mind of the creator.

On a spiritual level, the half-clear crystal can be the beginning of wisdom. If it knows that it doesn't know, it will turn to heaven for support and knowledge. If, however, it sits in its arrogance, trying to limit God to its own conception, this is worse than complete ignorance. To a certain extent, we are all under the half-clear energy. We don't and can't know God completely, and it is best not to be too dogmatic about our own beliefs or too scornful about those of others.

Silent stone

The silent stone looks rather like an egg, with its smooth, rounded shape and its opaque whiteness. In its fragility, its protectiveness, and its great potential, it is like an egg in more ways than its appearance. Like an egg, it can go bad if it's held too long and will break if it is stepped on. The silent stone's problems are overeagerness and overcaution. Both kill whatever potential is there. Timing is absolutely crucial for the silent stone, more so than for any other stone.

On a physical level the silent stone is associated with new ideas and events. No one can ever wipe out the past and make a clean start — the commonest myth of childhood — but there are ways to learn from and accept the past, and thus to avoid repeating it. The silent stone offers new projects and ideas, but you must be ready for them, or they will go the way of the last set of New Year's resolutions. The way to prepare for new ideas is not just to wait, though waiting does have its part; you must wait, pray, analyze the mistakes of the past, try to curb your impatience or liven your caution. You must concentrate on the new project, and be willing to forgive yourself for mistakes — and then go on.

Moreover, you must be ready to protect your new ideas or new life from the sneers of the critics. That's why the stone is called silent; it waits until the new idea or life is fully hatched and able to protect itself before announcing its arrival. The silent stone usually appears in a reading when the new idea is just beginning to make itself known to you; it signals a time of preparation, not the time of announcement.

On a psychological level, timing is the key to the silent stone. The Greek word *kairos* precisely expresses the concept of finding the right time. It is more than simply a convenient time; it is the time appointed by the heavens for doing something. Some astrologers will analyze the best time to get married, start a new business, or take other important new steps, but *kairos* depends as much on the self as on the stars. You have to be prepared to take the risk right then. *Kairos* is not always obvious; sometimes the world rushes in on you and you simply have to deal with it immediately, without planning. Only in the light of later events do you realize that the changes that seemed forced on you were made at the critical time.

Here is the best example of *kairos* I know: A young woman

for whom I've done many readings chose or was forced to change her life completely. She found it necessary to leave the city — even the state — she loved, learn skills she had been resisting for years, change her job, separate from her circle of friends, and end a longterm but fruitless relationship. In less than six months she had made the change completely and was happy, enjoying her new skills and sense of competence, forming a new circle of friends while still attached to the old. She had also met the man she would later marry. Recognizing *kairos*, she had left a dying and destructive life in which she had ceased to grow and made herself a new life that has had rewards beyond her dreams.

On a spiritual level, the silent stone heralds a new life. The egg is the symbol of Easter and the resurrection; we too are resurrected, in greater and lesser ways, throughout our lives and beyond. Cherish and protect your new beginning, knowing also that new life is always preceded by labor pains.

Montana agate

Montana agate — a translucent stone flecked with dark places — is an apt symbol of problems from the past. The past can chain us more effectively than anything else. If not transformed by forgiveness and understanding, old humiliations, old failures, old suffering can cripple new projects and ideas. The shadow of Montana agate is fear, restraint, and lack of forgiveness of yourself and others.

On a physical level Montana agate signifies a chance to deal with the problems of the past. This is good news, though it probably won't seem like it at the time. Under its influence, you can correct past mistakes, forgive yourself and others for long-past trespasses, and correct your vision of what actually happened. (You may have been suffering over a complete misunderstanding all these years.) Often, old loves or estranged relatives, especially siblings, will be coming back into your life, perhaps only briefly, and you'll have a chance to make some kind of reconciliation with them.

On a psychological level, Montana agate brings up old nightmares and worries from the past. There are two common reasons for this distressing development: you may be going through (or will soon be going through) a situation similar in structure or emotional content to the past experience, or you are psychologically ready to deal with the old hurt. If you find yourself thinking or dreaming about a painful past situation, you should ask yourself if it reminds you of a current situation. If it does in any way, you can learn from the mistakes of the past and perhaps exorcise that bad memory. Depending on its seriousness, you may want to talk it over with a counselor, therapist, or pastor; it's also helpful to write about it in a journal, perhaps visualizing ways things could have been different and better.[9] If there is no apparent reason for the memory to be pestering you, it could even be that this is an anniversary of the incident. Most likely, you are simply ready to work on the problem; these things always seem to come up when you are emotionally strong enough to handle them.

On a spiritual level, Montana agate helps you forgive the past (again, both yourself and others) in order to get on with the present. Once you have forgiven, the pain of the past will be transformed into a bridge between you and those who have suffered through similar problems; you can help others because you yourself have survived. Montana agate can help you avoid repeating the past and give you compassion for others who are in trouble.

Smoky Quartz

Smoky quartz (like rose quartz and amethyst) is a quartz crystal with some additional minerals that color it. Though the colored quartzes don't have the flawless purity of clear quartz crystal, they do have its strength and insight. Smoky quartz is a dramatic stone with a range of potentialities. At its best, it can be supremely creative; at its worst, it is full of self-blame and even self-hatred, and it can have the hasty temper of the oversensitive.

On a physical level smoky quartz is a now-you-see-it, now-you-don't magic act. It conceals itself beneath layers of mystery.

Whether it's a game or a serious attempt at camouflage is not always easy to tell. It indicates a desire for mystery and excitement, and it also represents the artistic temperament. Smoky quartz influences actors and writers who try on different personas, whether they are adopting these personas for the sake of their art, for fun, or to protect a frightened and fragile self.

On a psychological level, smoky quartz is not always dramatic (though it can be). People who are protecting themselves often do so by blending in with the crowd, rather than trying to stand out. Indeed, this stone's energy often applies to teenagers who wish they were less brilliant and unusual than they are. (They often discover that in college, the brilliant and unusual are more easily accepted than in high school.)

On a spiritual level, smoky quartz represents the self looking for a way that seems to be hidden from the seeker. Though the spirit is willing to travel along the Path, the Path itself seems unclear. Sometimes the desire is present, but the Path seems impossible to take, and the self will go on fruitlessly looking for another way. At other times, the Path itself is not clear at all and the only remedy is prayer, meditation, waiting, and searching through talking with others and reading spiritual works.

Onyx

Onyx deals with courage and rebirth. Its positive aspect is associated with extraordinary strength. Its shadow side, however, can show up as incorrigible sulkiness, as the self refuses to try or to enjoy anything for fear it will be taken away.

On a physical level onyx symbolizes strength: strength during suffering, and the strength that comes from having suffered and endured. It is not necessarily stoic; it may weep and share its miseries, but it doesn't run away, it doesn't give up, and it doesn't ignore its troubles. It looks them straight in the eye, and it endures. No other virtue is much good without this brand of endurance and courage. Onyx's stubborn persistence is helpful in any situation.

Sometimes its best expression is in waiting things out; at other times it demands action. Persistence, courage, and endurance are not always passive qualities.

On a psychological level, onyx indicates reaching the root of a problem. The courage needed to face inner demons is at least as great as that which is needed on a battlefield. Long struggles with self-doubt, loneliness, humiliation, and pain give you the strength to deal with many other kinds of problems. It also suggests a kind of humor, the wild laughter of those who have suffered unimaginable things — battlefield or gallows humor, even the humor of the operating room.

On a spiritual level, onyx signifies rebirth after a period of dryness and sorrow. Onyx honors the courageous. Those who have endured what St. John of the Cross called the dark night of the soul know the joy that the first refreshing streams bring.[10]

Notes

1. Matthew 5:5. *The New American Standard Bible* (Chicago: Moody Press, 1975).

2. Eric Doyle, *St. Francis and the Song of Brotherhood* (New York: Seabury Press, 1981), pp. 9-10.

3. *Devotions upon Emergent Occasions*, Meditation XVII, in *John Donne, Poetry and Prose*, edited by Frank J. Warnke (New York: Modern Library, 1967). Biographical information is from pp. xxvi-xxxii.

4. Matthew 12:25.

5. Luke 17:21.

6. For an excellent discussion of the role of discipline in the spiritual life, see C. S. Lewis, *The Screwtape Letters and Screwtape Proposes a Toast* (New York: Macmillan, 1961), pp. 13, 36-39.

7. Matthew 6:34.

8. Matthew 10:16.

9. A useful book on the process of journal keeping is Ira Progoff's *At a Journal Workshop* (New York: Dialogue House Library, 1975). Progoff's Intensive Journal (R) Workshops are held around the country; the book is the text for them, in case you cannot get to one. For techniques of visualization, see Shakti Gawain, *Creative Visualization* (New York: Bantam, 1978).

10. St. John of the Cross, *Dark Night of the Soul*, translated by E. Allison Peers (Garden City, NY: Image Books, 1959).

3

The Role of Colors

Colors are an integral part of the interpretations of *The Crystal Tree*. Both the colors of the stones and of the sephiroth have meaning; in fact, when you first are learning to interpret a new stone, the color is the most important factor to consider.

A great deal of work has been done on color theory, most of it from a psychological point of view.[1] In general, modern color interpretations agree with the traditional ones, which is surprising until you consider that color theory is descriptive, not prescriptive. The effect of color is observed and described in modern as well as traditional color theory, and the ancients were at least as able to observe and describe as we are today.

The Meanings of the Colors

Red

Red is traditionally the color of passion, action, and emotion. As the lowest-frequency color on the spectrum, it is the nearest of all colors to the other physical senses. Directly below it on the scale of vibrations is heat; below that is sound. Though it often is associated solely with war (Mars, the planet of war, is the red planet), it is also the color of valentines and of love. In Russia and China, red has always been considered lucky: it is the color of life and hope.[2] Red Square, in Moscow, has always been called so; it did not change its name when the Bolsheviks (whose color was and is red) took over. In heraldry red signifies magnanimity and fortitude;[3] both are qualities of the heart, which pumps red blood. In *The Crystal Tree*, red is the color of the sephirah Crown.

Orange

Orange is a color of intelligence and sharing. In China and Japan, it is considered the color of love. It contains the vitality of red and the intellect of yellow (the two colors that are combined to make orange). Orange is often associated with gold, which in ancient Greece was considered the link between the heavens and the earth.[4] Orange is considered exuberant and inventive.[5]

In *The Crystal Tree*, two shades of orange are considered: the dark orange known as bittersweet, which belongs to the sephirah Wisdom and is less exuberant and more thoughtful, and the bright orange of the sephirah Understanding, which is gregarious and lively.

Yellow

Pure, bright yellow is a cheerful and intelligent color. It is the color of sunlight, many early spring flowers, and ripe grain. Yellow is devoted to spiritual progress. Buddhist monks' robes are tinted yellow with the precious herb saffron. In heraldry, yellow signifies faith, constancy, and glory.[6] Interestingly, though bright yellow is a universally positive color, dark yellow is considered the color of treachery, even of Judas.

In *The Crystal Tree*, bright yellow is the color of the sephirah Mercy.

Brown

Brown, the color of the earth itself, is a solid and strong color that some people find unexciting. In Christian symbolism, it signifies the self's dying to worldly things and repentence from sin.[7] It is the color of the desert and of solitude, two attributes of the religious life. Brown's plain strength makes it honest and straightforward, but the color shows its best side when combined with one of the brighter colors, such as the yellow of Mercy, the orange of Understanding, even the bittersweet of Wisdom.

In *The Crystal Tree*, brown — a rich, fertile golden brown — is associated with the sephirah Severity.

Green

Green is the earth's color of life, the color of resurrection and of abundance. Its symbolism is obviously derived from the greening of the countryside in the spring. In heraldry, green signifies love and joy.[8] The connection with love may explain why jealousy is sometimes associated with this color.

In *The Crystal Tree*, green is associated with the sephirah Beauty. Beauty is the product of a balance between Mercy and Severity; the green of spring is the product of both sunlight and the dark earth.

Blue

Blue is a color of heaven: an easy connection to make, since the sky (where the heavens are usually considered to be located) is blue. Therefore, in every culture, blue is the color of hope, piety, and sincerity. In heraldry blue signifies chastity, loyalty, and fidelity.[9] The Celts considered it the color of a poet or bard.[10]

In *The Crystal Tree*, there are two shades of blue: the rich azure of the sephirah Victory, which governs mature love and commitment, self-discipline, and self-expression through art, and the deep blue of the sephirah Splendor, which governs children, work, and rewards.

Purple

Purple is a royal color in cultures as diverse and scattered as the ancient Roman, the Aztec, and the modern Western.[11] Perhaps because kings or lords were also judges, purple is associated with justice as well. Its heraldic association is with temperance, though purple is the color of wine.[12] Shades of purple are also linked with psychic and creative work, with a special sensitivity to ideas and impressions, and with a state of half-mourning.

In *The Crystal Tree*, there are two shades of purple. Violet (associated with psychic and spiritual sensitivity) belongs to the sephirah Foundation, which represents the realm of the spirit; deep imperial purple (associated with royalty and justice) belongs to Kingdom, which is the expression of the order of the Universe and the majesty of all creation.

Notes

1. See, for example, Max Lüscher, *The Lüscher Color Test*, translated and edited by Ian A. Scott (New York: Washington Square Press, 1969).

2. J.C. Cooper, *An Illustrated Encyclopaedia of Traditional Symbols* (London: Thames and Hudson, 1978), p. 40.

3. *Brewer's Dictionary of Phrase and Fable: Centenary Edition*, revised by Ivor H. Evans (New York: Harper and Row, 1970), p. 249.

4. Cooper, p. 40.

5. Walter B. Gibson and Litzka R. Gibson, *The Complete Illustrated Book of the Psychic Sciences* (New York: Bantam, 1968), p. 105.

6. Brewer, p. 249.

7. Cooper, p. 40.

8. Brewer, p. 249.

9. Brewer, p. 249.

10. Cooper, p. 40.

11. Cooper, p. 40.

12. Brewer, p. 249.

4

The Tree of Life

The Tree of Life is one of the most ancient symbols. It stood by the Tree of Knowledge in the Garden of Eden; it stands on both sides of the river of living water in the New Jerusalem.[1] According to the Kabbala, it is the "divine and deifying spirit," the manifestation of "pure and unitive grace."[2] The fruit of the Tree of Life is wholeness, that state of union with God in which God's will is our peace;[3] but beyond that, it stands for the primal wholeness of unfallen creation, before death entered the world. At its highest level, the Tree of Life represents the wholeness of God, and each sephirah — each branch, so to speak — symbolizes a different aspect of the Divine.

The symbolic representation of the Tree of Life (see Figure 4.1.) is taken from the Kabbala, the ancient Jewish mystical lore that has been called "the Jewish branch of that universal tree of deifying wisdom."[4] In other words, the Kabbala (and its symbol, the Tree of Life) is one expression of an overwhelming universal truth. "God has revealed these mysteries in many traditional or religious forms; but this diversity is only the expression of the infinite richness of the one truth."[5] Though many other cultures use

Figure 4.1 The Tree of Life

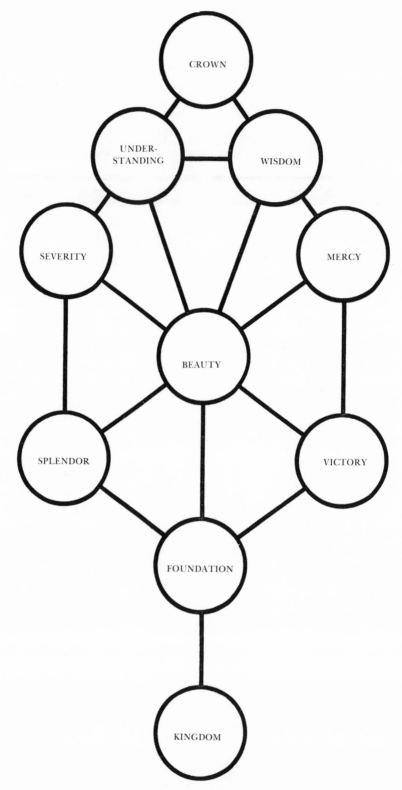

the symbol of the tree, the Kabbalistic symbol is structured in a way that makes it ideal for divination; this structure is already familiar to many tarot readers as a spread. So the framework of the *The Crystal Tree* is a physical symbol of a universal truth; do not confuse the representation (the lines and circles and even the interpretations) with the Tree itself, which is transcendant, invisible, and beyond our understanding.

The Kabbalistic Tree of Life is only one tree in myth and religion. Druidical tradition holds trees sacred; there are holy trees in Greek and Norse and even Buddhist mythologies. (I recently read that the tree under which the Buddha found enlightenment is suffering from the smoke of pilgrims' candles.) The tree symbol crosses all cultural boundaries. Trees are found in the heavens of religions of the ancient Sumerians, the Japanese, and the Christians. The tree is described as

> joining the three worlds and making communication between them possible. . . . Rooted in the depth of the earth, at the world centre, and in contact with the waters, the tree grows into the world of Time, adding rings to manifest its age, and its branches reach the heavens and eternity.[6]

Because the tree is a bridge between heaven and earth, it has its earthly meanings as well as its high and holy ones. The Tree of Life, as used in *The Crystal Tree*, deals with three levels of human existence: physical, psychological, and spiritual. Each of the ten branches, or sephiroth, of the Tree of Life can be interpreted as a step or part of human life. Physically, the sephiroth represent growth from birth to preparation for death and the afterlife. Psychologically, they represent the ascending spiral of growth and change from the first realization of oneself as a separate person to the death-and-regeneration experiences of self-transformation. Spiritually, the Tree of Life is a model of the individual quest for God.

Sephirah	Number	Stone	Pillar	Major Arcana
Crown	One	Rose quartz Red cullet	Moderation	The Magician Strength
Wisdom	Two	Red jasper	Mercy	The High Priestess The Hanged Man
Understanding	Three	Carnelian	Severity	The Empress Death
Mercy	Four	Cat's-eye	Mercy	The Emperor Temperance
Severity	Five	Brown agate	Severity	The Hierophant The Devil
Beauty	Six	Aventurine Green quartz	Moderation	The Lovers The Tower
Victory	Seven	Hematite	Mercy	The Chariot The Star
Splendor	Eight	Sodalite	Severity	Justice The Moon
Foundation	Nine	Chevron amethyst	Moderation	The Hermit The Sun
Kingdom	Ten	Amethyst	Moderation	Wheel of fortune Judgment

Figure 4.2 The Sephiroth and Their Correspondences

Sephirah	Color	Element	Planet	Key Word
Crown	Red	Fire	Sun	Self
Wisdom	Bittersweet	Water	Moon	Insight
Understanding	Orange	Air	Mercury	Communication
Mercy	Yellow	Earth	Venus	Self-esteem
Severity	Golden brown	Fire	Mars	Struggle
Beauty	Green	Water	Jupiter	Balance
Victory	Blue	Air	Saturn	Discipline/ desire
Splendor	Indigo	Earth	Uranus	Rewards
Foundation	Violet	Water/Fire	Neptune	Faith
Kingdom	Purple	Earth/Air	Pluto	Regeneration

So the Tree of Life is both a symbol of human life and a metaphor for the Path. In all its levels and shades of meaning, the Tree of Life is a symbolic (not rational), metaphoric (not literal) representation of a truth that cannot be approached or explained rationally and literally. As is true of any symbol, a very small figure represents a huge and overshadowing truth. Don't confuse the mundane interpretations of the Tree — even the spiritual interpretations — with the mighty philosophical and theological truths of the Tree of Life as set forth in the Kabbala; the aspects of the Divine presence are far above the tasks of daily life, though God can bless those tasks and make them holy. Likewise, in any metaphor, a true thing is compared to or called something else, in order to illumine its nature. To paraphrase Picasso, metaphors are lies that tell the truth.[7] Metaphors are mirrors to reflect unexpected angles of an elusive face. The mirror is not the face itself; nor is a mirror really a metaphor, but it does illumine a difficult meaning.

On a more practical level, the Tree of Life is the structure on which *The Crystal Tree* is patterned: an arrangement of ten sephiroth, each dealing with a different area of life, on which stones are placed. The interplay between a stone's meaning and the influence of the sephirah provides interpretations that are useful in divination.

To better understand the divinations, the Tree of Life itself must be studied and understood. The Tree of Life has patterns of meaning and structure in addition to the meaning of the individual sephiroth. Below, I give the interpretations of the sephiroth first, including the meanings for divination; the patterns of the Tree of Life are examined next. The sephiroth are listed in order, from the first to the tenth, but the tree itself is always presented root upward: that is, Crown, the first sephirah reading from the top downward, is the root of the tree. To climb, one must go downward; the inverted tree symbolizes Divine wisdom flowing from heaven.[8]

For a quick glance at each sephirah's meanings and associated colors, elements, planets, etc., see Figure 4.2.

The interpretations of the sephiroth are presented below in two ways. The section immediately following is a brief encapsulation of the the sephiroth's meanings. After this key, I offer more detailed and in-depth interpretations, which are a bit esoteric and may not be easily comprehensible to all readers. However, I hope you will read this section, since a deeper understanding of the Tree and of the sephiroth will greatly enhance your Crystal Tree readings. You should at least look at the last paragraph of the interpretation of each sephirah, because the last paragraph explains how the sephirah should be interpreted in different kinds of readings.

A Guide to the Sephiroth

Crown

In Hebrew, Kether. Crown symbolizes pure energy, the self, individuality, growth, ambition.

Wisdom

In Hebrew, Chokmah. Wisdom represents instinctive knowing, the dark side, the unconscious, balance and imbalance, the object of a search, motives.

Understanding

In Hebrew, Binah. Understanding relates to primary emotional ties, relations with family and friends, social life.

Mercy

In Hebrew, Chesed. Mercy (also translated as Grace) signifies hope, areas of comfort and solidity, gifts and strengths, positive qualities.

Severity

In Hebrew, Din or Geburah. Severity (also translated as Judgment) indicates fears, areas of struggle and risk, drawbacks, restraints, problems.

Beauty

In Hebrew, Tiphareth. Beauty symbolizes balance, harmony, creative energy, health, the physical body.

Victory

In Hebrew, Netzach. Victory relates to discipline and desire, limits and drives, romantic love, commitment, the intellect, art, and creativity.

Splendor

In Hebrew, Hod. Splendor signifies rewards and results, work, money, children, craftsmanship.

Foundation

In Hebrew, Yesod. Foundation represents the structure of the soul, spiritual life and relationships, psychic work.

Kingdom

In Hebrew, Malkuth. Kingdom is associated with the physical Universe, the shape of a life, the ultimate outcome of a problem, earthly success.

More Complete Interpretations of the Sephiroth

Crown

Crown is the root of the inverted tree: the first step for the soul. It symbolizes the unalterable center of the personality; though the body grows and ages and the mind learns and forgets, the spirit — Crown — remains. Crown's ruling planet, the Sun, is the obvious choice for this glowing, indomitable center of the self: of all the heavenly bodies in our solar system, only the Sun is steady, unvarying, not subject to waxing and waning. Even changes in the length of the days are not changes in the Sun itself, but steps in its minuet with the Moon — whose light, of course, is reflected sunlight.

Crown belongs to the element fire and the color red. Crown's fire is the unconsuming flame of pure spirit; it is creative, not destructive, and runs as sap or blood or magma through every living thing. Its red is the red of flame and heat. You cannot gaze at the Sun or sleep on a bed of hot coals; neither can you grasp Crown except fleetingly, for its intensity is too great. Pure essence is not of this world. Once Crown finds a channel of expression, the channel itself becomes what is read and interpreted, and Crown has once more managed to hide itself. Perhaps hide is the wrong word; Crown wants to manifest itself, to strike life into the lifeless, to drive and inspire, and those things can only be done from within. So Crown slips into its vessel and becomes, not a forest fire consuming its victims from the outside, but a lamp, a hearth, a sacred flame.

In divination, Crown represents the essence of a problem. In a character reading, it is the salient point of a character. The two stones that belong to the sephirah Crown are rose quartz and red cullet; they represent two kinds of selves. Rose quartz, despite its pallor and its seeming delicacy, is a stone of great strength. It represents the will at peace with itself and with others. Red cullet has clarity, vigor, and flair; unlike rose quartz, however, it is not at peace, and its will is active, asserting itself over others.

Wisdom

Wisdom emanates from Crown; along with the next sephirah, Understanding, Wisdom shows the primary expression of Crown's pure flame. More subtle and less self-absorbed than Crown, Wisdom is aware of the outside world: Wisdom's chief role is to translate the outside world into symbols and images. Though perceptive, Wisdom is not perceived; it watches in stealth and delivers its images through dreams and daydreams, scents, images, gestures, stray notes of music. It is instinctive, not rational, and it does not express itself in words. Wisdom is the source for all the arts as well as for nightmares. (The poet and the philistine may have similar faculties of Wisdom, but the poet listens to Wisdom and strives to express it, while the philistine tries hard to stop the persistent voice that keeps whispering strange insights.)

The Moon rules Wisdom. Unlike the Sun, the Moon is aware, watchful, subtle. The Moon's cycles enable it to understand things that change: emotions, growing plants, lives that begin and end. Crown is eternal and does not understand death or birth; Wisdom interprets both. The changes ruled by the Moon (and Wisdom) are not random or violent, but the predictable cycles of life. The pulse and the tides are sisters. They seek balance through change; they achieve rhythm. Wisdom signifies the search for balance, the sense of that rhythm.

Wisdom is related to water and the color bittersweet. The underground streams and lakes that rise into wells and springs are an apt metaphor for the secret workings of Wisdom. So is water's variability, its ability to take on any shape and carry any freight, from microscopic grains of sand to whales and ocean liners. Bittersweet is a color midway between orange and red; it reflects Wisdom's role as the mediator, carrier of messages between two worlds.

In divination, Wisdom refers to motives, imagination, instincts, and to the object of a search. Because it is dual, it reveals both the object (the sought-for) and the subject (what drives you to seek). In a character reading, this sephirah indicates how instinctive wisdom is operating and whether it is valued. The stone associated with Wisdom is red jasper, a fine-grained, opaque, secret stone that denotes restlessness and passion.

Understanding

Understanding represents a primary expression of Crown. Unlike Wisdom, it does not watch and listen in secret; instead it presents itself openly through communication. Understanding is logical, structured, literate. Though it is more open than Wisdom, Understanding, unlike Crown, has the ability to lie. Understanding influences not only the basic way we communicate with others but also the messages we find easiest — or impossible — to send. We learn what is acceptable and what is forbidden almost as soon as we learn to talk, and from the same people: our family members (whether or not we are biologically related to them). Since relationships — whether familial, friendly, or romantic — are based on communication, Understanding also rules families, social life, friendships, love (not marriage, though communication in marriage is strongly affected by Understanding), and attitudes toward strangers and those of other backgrounds. By extension, it also rules our receptivity to new ideas and influences.

The planet Mercury is connected with Understanding. Mercury's quickness makes it the cosmic messenger; in its incarnations as Hermes and Thoth, Mercury is credited with inventing books, medicine, divination, and theft. Mercury can never be more than 28 degrees from the Sun,[9] because it is the voice of the Sun. (The Moon is its eyes and imagination.)

Understanding relates to the element air and the color orange. Air is the primary vehicle of conscious communication, from voices (modulated air) to radio and television waves sent through the air. Body language is largely an unconscious communication and belongs to the element earth, which rules our bodies. Writing is a very airy concept: translating sounds into shapes is a fanciful intellectual exercise, ideally suited to air. The color orange seems cheerful and pleasant because it is the color of sharing, conversation, and communication. Orange is a highly social color, often used to decorate restaurants, bars, student lounges in colleges, and other places that are meant to be social centers.

In divination, the sephirah Understanding reveals relations with family and friends, social life, and your ability to communicate. The carnelian, a translucent orange stone, belongs to Understanding and indicates warmth of heart and clarity of intellect.

Mercy

The sephirah Mercy is associated with self-esteem, positive qualities, and areas of strength. Mercy — also translated as Grace — does not mean an egotistically high opinion of yourself, not haughtiness or pride. It is, instead, the humble willingness to see and accept the good in yourself and in others.[10] It is the basic acceptance of your own existence. Without Mercy even the most brilliant Crown is lost, because it will not believe in its own worth.

The planet Venus fittingly rules Mercy, because, although Venus is associated with love, it is more than a planet of passion. Venus rules love of all kinds. Loving your neighbor as yourself — perhaps even loving God with all your heart and soul and mind — requires that you love yourself first.[11] If you can forgive yourself, it is easier to forgive others; the more you go on loving and respecting yourself, the more you will be able to reach out to others in love. When in turn they love you back, your self-love will increase and you will be able to love them more. This love cycle has great potential and power, if only you will let it begin. But first you must learn Mercy.

Mercy belongs to the element earth and the color yellow. Too often earth is considered a materialistic and greedy element; though it can be distorted in those ways, earth is also what we are truly made of. Animated by fire, breathing air, veins running water in its guise of blood, we are apt to forget that from dust we came and to dust we will return. We are part of the natural cycle; when we divorce ourselves from it, we become sick and destructive. Earth rules the flesh and can control or forgive its weaknesses; we sometimes lose sight of Mercy when we forget we are animals and condemn in ourselves what flesh is heir to. Moreover, since Mercy begins to be determined when we are very young, if our parents often condemned us for earthiness (for the noisy play of all young creatures, for our bodily functions, or our need for attention), we may find it hard to accept and enjoy ourselves, and Mercy is lost.

The color yellow is connected with this sephirah. Yellow, the color of sunlight, spring flowers, cheer, joy, is also the color of Buddhist monks' robes: a clearsighted color that represents new life.

In divination, Mercy indicates the strengths of a certain position, your best qualities, and the source of your power. In a character reading, this sephirah shows your attitude towards forgiveness and self-forgiveness, your quality and type of self-esteem. Cat's-eye, the stone that belongs to Mercy, signifies the clearsightedness that sees both good and bad yet still tries to think the best of everything.

Severity

Severity is not Mercy's opposite but its companion. The two work together to create a whole personality. Severity is not self-hatred, but realistic self-assessment, and it supplies the energy to make changes when needed. Without the struggles and daring of Severity, we would never know our own strength. Moreover, Severity — the ability to see our own faults and change them — is as necessary to a balanced personality as Mercy is.

The planet Mars rules Severity, because aggression's proper place is in beginning new ventures, enduring hardships, and struggling against evil and troubles. Though Mercy is the first step in change (providing the ground to stand on, so to speak) Severity is the initiator of change. The Mercy/Severity cycle works much like the love cycle discussed previously. First, Mercy gives enough self-respect so that you value yourself and want to change bad habits and win old battles. Severity then gives the impetus to change these habits and confers the anger and strength necessary to conquer enemies. Once the struggle is done, Mercy takes over again and allows total forgiveness, of yourself and the others involved. The resultant increase in self-esteem may allow you to tackle another bad habit or old battle.

Severity belongs to the element fire, and its color is golden brown. Fire in its fierce aspect can clear the way for new building as no other element can: rapidly, thoroughly, cleanly. Golden brown combines the sturdiness of brown with a lighter, richer note and promises hope and renewed fertility — once those weeds are out of the way!

In divination, the sephirah Severity indicates areas of fear and weakness, areas where strength will be required. (The stones in Mercy and Severity almost always have a strong relationship, because our strengths and our weaknesses mirror one another.) Brown agate belongs to Severity; it emphasizes the endurance and guts necessary to make changes and to improve yourself.

Beauty

Beauty is the balance between Mercy and Severity and suggests the health of someone with both self-esteem and humility. Balance is the basis for both health and happiness. Balance comes through having the right priorities and keeping life in perspective. But Beauty is more than a chilly equilibrium. Once in balance, all Beauty wants to do is explore, enjoy, embrace. It is exuberant, bursting with health and vitality, not yet subject to restrictions or responsibilities. Yet the choices Beauty makes are vital.

The planet Jupiter is associated with Beauty; Jupiter is best known astrologically as the greater benefic, the bestower of blessings. Astrologer Robert Hand has identifed its energies as being specifically energies of expansion and integration.[12] Beauty is clearly integrative as a balance between Mercy and Severity. Beauty's other role — that of expansion — involves taking the freedom that comes from maturity and balance, and simply enjoying it. Beauty suggests more than a calm demeanor; it represents the rich, vibrant exploration of life that only becomes possible when you can forgive your own mistakes (Mercy) and can afford to take risks (Severity).

Beauty is connected with the element water and the color green. Water, in seeking its own level, is both restless, ever-moving and restful, looking for equilibrium. Water is essential to the color green; nothing is so green as a rain forest, nothing so lacking in green as a desert. Beauty's lush enjoyment of its own vitality is as refreshing as spring flowers.

In divination, the sephirah Beauty indicates physical health, mental and emotional balance, as well as any possible overwork or irresponsibility. In a character reading, it will reveal your general health and your attitude toward the body and the home. The stones that belong to Beauty are aventurine and green quartz. Aventurine deals with the physical aspects of Beauty: health, attitude toward the body, and sexuality. Green quartz deals with the metaphysical aspects of Beauty: the balance of Mercy and Severity, guilt, irresponsibility, nerves, nightmares — essentially, whether the mind, body, soul, and spirit are working in harmony or are at odds.

Victory

Victory is the balance beyond balance. Beauty represents personal, inner balance; Victory balances the world and the self, relationships with others and privacy, responsibility and freedom, discipline and desire. Victory is the sephirah of romantic love and of marriage and commitment, of artistic and scientific creation, of self-expression and solitude. Though this sephirah may seem full of contradictions, it is necessary to master Victory in order to lead a full and responsible life. When this part is out of balance, your life is pressured by too many demands and you have no space; or, you may retreat from responsibility and from love, becoming lonely, unwilling to make a commitment, cynical about the opposite sex, and/or promiscuous (enjoying sex without making any kind of commitment).

In order to have a strong Victory, you don't have to be married or involved in a permanent romantic relationship. You do need an appropriate balance of giving and accepting in all relationships with other people; a sense of responsibility towards yourself and others; a willingness to make and keep commitments, whether that commitment is to an art, a job, a hobby, another person, yourself.

The planet Saturn is associated with Victory. Saturn has a reputation for being a cosmic spoilsport, but recently astrologers have turned their attention to its positive roles.[13] Saturn's energies are disciplinary and restraining, and it is not surprising that they are unpopular in cultures that equate discipline with violence and restraint with repression. Discipline is not imposed from without, but grows from within, from the balance of priorities achieved in Beauty. Restraint, likewise, is not repression but a careful judgment of what is destructive and what is constructive. Freedom without restraint rapidly turns into excess.

Victory is connected with the element air and the color blue. Air is both communicative and detached; its logic and clarity of thought are needed to make judgments — implicit in Victory. One of Victory's chief roles is self-expression. Self-expression results from air's disposition to communicate combined with Saturnine discipline. Blue, the classic color of heaven, is the color of air, ideas, and thought.

In divination, the sephirah Victory indicates both romance and responsibility. In a character reading, it reveals how you reconcile love and duty. The stone associated with Victory is hematite, which signifies committed love, transformation through self-discipline, and unconditional devotion to God.

Splendor

Splendor is the harvest, the reward, so to speak, of all the sephiroth that came before it. It deals with money, children, work, inventions, mastery after apprenticeship, and all the results and rewards of work.

Uranus rules Splendor, a planetary connection that may seem odd at first. Traditionally, Uranus is associated with the sudden, the strange, the ultra-modern. What is it doing in such traditional areas as children and money? For one thing, both children and money behave in unexpected ways; you cannot predict just what direction your children (or your mutual funds) are going to take, though there is often a kind of justice to their actions and decisions. They are the result of what you have sown, and not every harvest is a harvest of abundance. And harvest itself is more than bringing in the sheaves; it indicates a total (if temporary) change in the way of living and working, as anyone who has ever lived on a farm can testify. Uranus rules the rebellion of the young and their breaking away from their parents.[14] Also, Splendor is associated with inventions, an area that is traditionally Uranian.

Splendor belongs to the element earth and to the color indigo; both are splendid in their rich abundance. The earth's role in Splendor is active. Having been seeded, cultivated, and cared for, the earth gives back in harvest far more than was put into it, assuming that the Uranian disruptive energies of nature — from volcanoes to hurricanes — have not interfered. The true source of wealth is always, ultimately, the earth, no matter how many middlemen and manufacturers intervene. The earth is also the source of indigo: a natural plant dye, a color of great depth, dignity, and splendor. This tint was used on blue jeans that, in the 1960s at least, signified rebellion and a desire for a more peaceful, earth-loving way of life — a bitter reward for the older generation's materialism and war-making. Indigo is also a color of the New World; it is not native to the Eastern Hemisphere.

In divination, the sephirah Splendor indicates your children, money, and work. In a character reading, it reveals your attitude toward change and what is being sown and therefore reaped. Sodalite, the stone associated with Splendor, signifies achievement and success.

Foundation

Foundation shows life after the harvest. It is intensely, almost exclusively spiritual; it has gone beyond materialism and the cause-and-effect attitude of Splendor. It is associated with spirituality, psychic work, and appreciation of the arts. This sephirah is structured not by exterior rules but by precepts, though the precepts may result in a voluntary assumption of rules for the sake of discipline.

The planet Neptune is connected with Foundation. Neptune, with its mysteriousness, its hazy impenetrability, is the ideal planet to be linked with the spiritual aspects of Foundation, but the intricate structure that Foundation perceives in the Universe may seem non-Neptunian. Yet Neptune rules the psychic — that is, the normally unnoticed substructure of all communication. It also is the idealistic planet. You could think of Neptune as a Neo-Platonist; it believes in ideal images (known as Ideas) of which our reality is only a dim and ruined reflection.[15] Neptune — and the sephirah Foundation — sees clearly the ideal structure of the cosmos that seems like an illusion to us.

Foundation is associated with two elements: water and fire. Both are instinctive, nonrational, and spiritual, attuned not to any practical or logical reality but to the invisible beauties of insight, instinct, passion, and emotion. Foundation's color is violet, a color that is both royal and psychic, a color of twilight and half-mourning for the world. Foundation is very near the end of the Tree of Life; the spiral is nearly finished; a new time will begin soon.

In divination, Foundation indicates spiritual and psychic values. In a character reading, it reveals the particular quality and form of the questioner's spiritual quest. The stone associated with

Foundation is chevron amethyst, an amethyst banded with pure quartz that represents the contact between the spiritual and the physical.

Kingdom

Kingdom is the grand culmination of the Tree of Life. It indicates final outcomes, success, the world. Kingdom is the last preparation for regeneration and the beginning of a new spiral. In this it works as closely with Foundation as Severity works with Mercy.

Pluto is connected with the sephirah Kingdom, because Pluto is the planet of regeneration. Both Pluto and Kingdom can be disruptive if not dealt with in the right spirit and at the proper time, as though an orchestra played the fourth movement of Beethoven's Ninth Symphony first instead of last; though it is the best-known part of the symphony, it cannot be taken out of its context without ruining the structure of the music. As for Pluto's relationship with Foundation, the two must be taken together, as a whole. Remember that Pluto is not always the ninth planet from the Sun; it sometimes crosses Neptune's orbit and becomes eighth. The two work together to transform.

Kingdom belongs to the elements earth and air. It has a sense of solid reality to it. Foundation perceives the intricate and superb structure of the Universe that is made complete and manifest in Kingdom. Kingdom's color, dark purple, has none of the tentative quality of Foundation's violet; it is unabashedly regal. Kingdom does, indeed, belong to a king; it brings to mind medieval society, in which each person's role was defined and exact, and all bowed to the king's authority. Kingdom's structure is like that, except that the chance quality of birth and fortune are eliminated; all things work together in their ordained places because they were created for those specific places; nothing is interchangeable, each part is unique. In this, the ultimate state of balance, we are ready to move into the next cycle.

In divination, Kingdom means the ultimate outcome of the

question (ultimate for the period of the reading, that is). In a character reading, Kingdom reveals your mission at this time. The stone associated with Kingdom, the amethyst, traditionally has been considered a protection against loss of control, loss of self. The amethyst has integrity and cannot lose its self.

Patterns in the Tree of Life

The sephiroth of the Tree of Life are placed in a very definite order. As noted above, they run from Crown, the first sephirah and the root of the Tree, to Kingdom, the tenth sephirah and the top of the Tree. In this section we will examine the progression of the sephiroth and the internal patterns of the Tree's structure: the repetition of three, the three pillars, and the root-and-branch pattern.

The Progression of the Sephiroth

Crown, the first sephirah, represents the whole self or the whole of everything, the center and beginning of all emanations. It can be thought of as the infant who, not yet realizing that others exist, believes that the breast, the crib, and the sunlight are all part of itself. When the infant becomes aware that the breast is, in fact, its mother's, it reaches the second sephirah: Wisdom. The infant cannot control anything, even itself. It cannot define or explain the powerful emotions that possess it; it can only cry. The infant is unaware of rational thinking and subject to dreams. Thus Wisdom represents the unconscious mind, the ancient feelings and frustrations that haunt us into later life, the dreams that are so inexplicable to an infant, and all other things that cannot be put into words.

Learning to talk brings the child into the third sephirah, Understanding. The emotional forces that were so strongly sensed and so impossible to express in Wisdom have now theoretically become expressible through words. However, Understanding is

more than talk (though based on communication); it also represents the family, with its rules and unstated assumptions, that define what may and may not be said, what will and will not be be-
lieved. All emotional relationships in the future are based on what
happens in Understanding; it is very difficult to learn to speak of
things forbidden from your childhood.

The next two sephiroth, Mercy and Severity, are so intimately
linked that it is difficult to separate them. They represent the parts
of a single process: coming to terms with the self. Mercy, the
fourth sephirah, is placed ahead of Severity because in normal development the child first understands strengths and talents; only
later will he/she learn the limitations of those talents. Moreover,
the self-esteem learned in Mercy is necessary for a truly effective
Severity; those unable to admit their faults are least secure in their
good qualities.

Once Mercy has established the child's self-esteem, Severity
can test, train, and discipline the child. Without Severity, Mercy
becomes egotism to the point of megalomania, and the child can
truly achieve nothing. Without Mercy, Severity becomes self-hatred and self-destruction. Lesser imbalances are less fateful. A bit
too much Mercy can result in vanity, procrastination, bragging,
laziness, and the conviction that no one else is ever right. A bit
too much Severity can terrify the child into never admitting that
he/she is wrong. It can create a workaholic adult tormented by
self-doubts even at the moment of greatest achievement, unable
to love him/herself or others, or someone who, prevented by
those self-doubts, never tries anything new or takes any emotional
or creative risk.

However, when these two sephiroth are in balance, the child
becomes a fully functional adult: able to discipline him/herself
and to take a day off, reasonably and realistically assessing his/her
own good and bad actions, and able to admit mistakes as easily as
triumphs. The child — now almost an adult — has reached the
sixth sephirah, Beauty. Beauty may be a confusing word: the beauty here is that of balance, of wholeness. Beauty synthesizes Mercy

and Severity; through balancing them comes a tremendous joy. Beauty wants to try its wings, change the world, plunge into excitement, fall in love. Beauty is the equivalent of that phase of life after the miseries of adolescence and before the responsibilities of marriage. This chronology is not to be taken too seriously; Beauty first appears in flashes in childhood and should reappear periodically — especially as spring fever — until death. Though we move our emphasis from sephirah to sephirah, each is always with us.

With the onset of responsibility comes Victory. For an adult, the first task is the complex balancing of discipline and desire in the sephirah Victory. That balance is most often exemplified as marriage, though other committed relationships (for example, of two lesbians or gay men not legally permitted to marry, of a celibate priest or nun to God, of an artist to art) are equally metaphors for the necessary lifelong commitment. Nor are we limited to a single commitment. There are artists, for instance, who have strong commitments to their mates, to their art, and to God. The idea here is of commitment to something that does not wait on your pleasure alone; of being willing to bend yourself to another's needs or will while maintaining your integrity; of keeping the right priorities; of doing necessary daily duties without becoming slave to them. Victory is Beauty in action; the theoretical balance of Mercy and Severity that come together in Beauty find expression here.

The natural result of Victory is Splendor. Splendor — the material, psychological, and spiritual rewards of Victory — is usually represented by children (also a natural result of the marriage metaphor so often used for Victory). Children are not the only rewards, however; the commitment of Victory results in pride of craft, money, a settled and beautiful home, a sense of accomplishment. Though Splendor is not entirely material — people achieve Splendor without ever owning anything, making money, or being famous — this sephirah does encompass many material rewards, simply because so many of the tasks in Victory are material tasks.

But you cannot rest on your laurels. Splendor gives way to

Foundation, the sephirah of spiritual completion. Though material considerations still exist, they become less important as the spiritual ones shine through. Foundation prepares us for regeneration by reminding us of higher things.

Finally, Kingdom is reached. This sephirah is regeneration itself; it rejoices in a glimpse of the intricate beauties of a created Universe. So far, so hard to reach, Kingdom is the final result, the new birth.

This explication of the progression of the sephiroth takes the individual from birth to reuniting with God, but the Tree of Life can also be seen in another light. Like Jacob's ladder, angels both ascend and descend this Tree; the sephiroth can be read from Kingdom up. In that case, Kingdom represents the created world; Foundation suggests the first inklings of spiritual values, which are rewarded by Splendor. Rewards, once again, prove to be not enough, and the pilgrim moves away from what is freely permitted in Splendor to a more ascetic and committed life in Victory. Beauty offers a balance between materialism and asceticism. From there the pilgrim moves into a harsher self-judgment and more stringent standards in Severity; thence to a more forgiving attitude in Mercy. Understanding offers clear communication with God, but the pilgrim is still dominated by rationalism and reliance on human ways. In Wisdom, adoring the Most High, the seeker begins to know the holy from inside. Finally, Crown is the ultimate Crown of glory: becoming all that God intended.

The Tree of Life leads us to individuality, to true personhood, and then to something beyond. The processes of growth as described here are clear, step-by-step progressions, but no one follows the Tree of Life so exactly; we move on half a dozen different levels at once and in both directions. All our lives we move backwards and forwards on the Tree, learning how to combine the separate and individual with the all-inclusive — what we knew before the Fall, and what we must try to relearn.

The Three Triads and Kingdom

The Tree of Life can be divided naturally into three triads and the sephirah Kingdom. The topmost triad of Crown-Wisdom-Understanding deals with the formation of the inner self: its sense of its own existence and purpose, its hidden assumptions about the world that it is neither conscious of nor willing to question, and its way of communicating with others.

The second triad, Mercy-Severity-Beauty, deals with the conscious results of the first triad. In other words, Mercy relates to the conscious sense of self and self-esteem, while Crown is connected with the unconscious or primal. Severity represents conscious standards and ideas about the world, while Wisdom is equated with the unconscious perception. Beauty indicates your conscious relation to others, whether balanced or not, while Understanding describes the unconscious communication between you.

If, for example, you unconsciously want a partner who will be cold and cruel, that is a problem of Understanding, which will attract and be attracted to cold, cruel people. The actual troubles resulting from this problem will be made manifest in Beauty (which rules falling in love and balances between mind and body), where you will keep finding that partners who at first seemed kind are, after all, cold and cruel.

The third triad, Victory-Splendor-Foundation, deals with action. The self — unconscious in Crown and conscious in Mercy — is expressed in Victory: expressed by art, by the commitments you make, by what is desired and what is restrained. Your perception of the world — unconscious in Wisdom, conscious in Severity — justifies itself by the harvest implicit in Splendor. Your ability to communicate — unconscious in Understanding, conscious in Beauty — is tested in Foundation, which rules psychic communications, appreciation of the arts, and prayer, as well.

Kingdom, standing alone, sums up the subconscious, the conscious, and the actions. Character is destiny: the preceding nine sephiroth lead inevitably to the destiny revealed in the tenth sephirah, Kingdom.

The Three Pillars

The Tree of Life, especially in the Kabbala, has three pillars: Mercy, Severity, and Moderation. (See Figure 4.3.) The three sephiroth on the far right of the Tree belong to Mercy: Wisdom, Mercy, and Victory. In divination, these sephiroth are to be interpreted with as much leniency as possible. Philosophically, they represent active and positive traits.

The three sephiroth on the far left of the Tree of Life belong to Severity: Understanding, Severity, and Splendor. In divination, they are to be interpreted with rigor and a fierce regard for justice and stringency. Philosophically, they represent negative and passive qualities.

The four sephiroth in the center belong to Moderation, receive precise interpretations in divination, and philosophically provide a balanced view of life.[16]

Root and Branch

There is one last pattern in the Tree of Life: the reduplication of itself. The trunk and branches of a tree are mirrored by its roots and rootlets; there is as much of a tree that is invisible as is visible. The turning point for the Tree of Life is the sephirah Beauty. The first five sephiroth can be regarded as the roots of the Tree or the inner self (who you are); the last five are the branches or outer self (what you do).

The two parts reflect one another. Crown, the essential self-image, is mirrored by Beauty, the expression of the self with others. Wisdom intuitively knows the self and the Other — everything and everyone outside yourself — and is the unconscious well of creativity; Victory expresses that knowledge and creativity in art or love. Understanding deals with parents and the birth family, Splendor with children and the created family. Mercy is the root and source of inner strength, the best qualities of heart and mind; Foundation is the expression of these in spiritual terms and in daily life. Severity demands that we transform ourselves and gives us the necessary energy and will to do the transforming; Kingdom is the regeneration demanded and achieved.

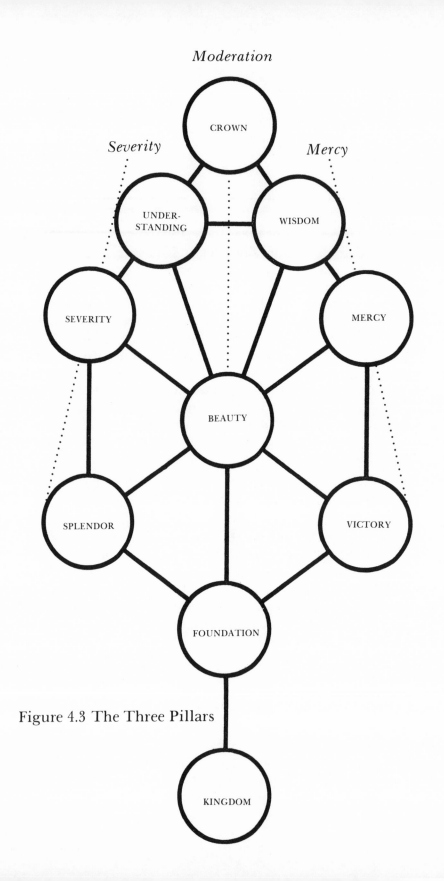

Figure 4.3 The Three Pillars

Notes

1. Genesis 2:9; Revelations 22:1-2.

2. Leo Schaya, *The Universal Meaning of the Kabbalah* (Baltimore, MD: Penguin, 1973), pp. 131, 134.

3. Ephesians 2:14.

4. Schaya, p. 19.

5. Schaya, p. 19.

6. J. C. Cooper, *An Illustrated Encyclopaedia of Traditional Symbols* (London: Thames and Hudson, 1978), p. 176. The role of the tree as bridge or path between heaven and earth is emphasized by its role in the myth of the Dying God: he always dies on a tree. Each of these myths — the stories of Osiris, Orpheus, Mithras, Odin, Baldur the Beautiful, and so many others — prefigures the death and resurrection of Christ, Who, in fulfilling the law, also fulfilled the ancient myth (really, the ancient prediction) of the god who would die in spring and resurrect Himself. All trees are made sacred by His death.

7. What Picasso reportedly said was, "Art is a lie that tells the truth."

8. Cooper, p. 176.

9. Alan Oken, *The Horoscope, the Road and Its Travelers* (New York: Bantam, 1974), p. 219.

10. C. S. Lewis, *The Screwtape Letters* (New York: Macmillan, 1961), pp. 62-65.

11. Matthew 22:37-40.

12. Robert Hand, *Horoscope Symbols* (Rockport, MA: Para Research, 1981), p. 65.

13. Hand, pp. 67-71; Donna Cunningham, *An Astrological Guide to Self-Awareness* (Reno, NV: CRCS, 1978), pp. 84-92.

14. Hand, p. 73.

15. Plato, *Republic*, section 596. The reflections — all the reality we can see — are known as Forms.

16. Traditional Kabbalistic literature assigns the negative pillar to the feminine, the positive to the masculine. I disagree with this analysis for several reasons. First, it makes no sense in terms of the meanings of the sephiroth — and of the planets that rule them. Wisdom, ruled by the Moon and ruling the unconscious, would seem "feminine," as would Mercy, ruled by Venus, though it rules self-esteem (not, alas, a traditionally feminine quality). Though Understanding, ruling family, might seem feminine, in what way would Severity, ruled by Mars and ruling aggression, be classically feminine? Such assignments seem forced and inaccurate. Second, this contradicts the traditional numerological assumption that odd numbers are masculine and even numbers are feminine (the sephiroth on the pillar of severity are numbered 3, 5, and 8; those on the pillar of mercy are 2, 4, and 7; the others are on the pillar of moderation). Since our numerological tradition is descended from the *gematria* — part of the Kabbala — the Kabbala essentially contradicts itself here. When I find ancient systems contradicting one another, it usually is over the masculine/feminine problem. Sometimes the ancients tried too hard to make both the world and the heavens reflect their own sexist perspective; I have discarded those remnants of patriarchal culture.

Part Three

How to Use The Crystal Tree

5

How to Use The Crystal Tree

Before you begin a reading, it's best to relax and develop your concentration. If you take plenty of time to prepare yourself, the reading will have more meaning. The more relaxed and tranquil you feel, the more easily and deeply you will interpret the stones.

You can prepare yourself by simply letting yourself become quiet, a process the Quakers call "centering down." As you sit, concentrating on quietness, you'll slowly settle into a peaceful near-trance state in which images and insights will swim to the surface of your consciousness. It's a floating feeling similar to the last stage before you fall asleep; if you make a sudden move or try to grab at a passing thought, you'll be jerked out of it. Gradually you'll be able to move and even talk without losing that sense of floating, and then you are ready.

There are other relaxation techniques you can use, too: yoga techniques, the Japanese tea ceremony, the preparations for karate, even a soothing bath. Do not drink alcohol or caffeine or take drugs before using *The Crystal Tree!* A single glass of wine might not hurt, but in general all artificial stimulants are distracting and ultimately destructive; even the tea ceremony is best done with a mild herbal tea, such as mint or lemon verbena. Ginseng is less desirable even than black tea, for it can raise your blood pressure.

To do a reading with *The Crystal Tree*, spread the Tree of Life board on a flat surface. Open the bag containing the stones. Close your eyes and meditate or concentrate on a specific question, person, or idea. Yes-or-no questions are not as good as open-ended questions. For example, instead of asking, Should I change my job?, concentrate on "career." Reach into the bag, choose a stone, and place it on the Tree of Life board. The first stone drawn should be placed on the first circle (*sephirah*, plural *sephiroth*), the second stone on the second sephirah, and so on until ten stones have been drawn and each sephirah has been filled.

How do you choose a stone? It will simply feel right in your hand. Each stone has a characteristic vibration, which your own psychic abilities can sense. If you look at the stones while you choose, your conscious mind will take over (especially once you know the meanings of the stones) and you'll find yourself controlling the outcome. It's better to relax and trust your psychic sense. To prevent peeking, you may want to make a cloth bag to hold the stones.

Once the stones are laid out, don't be too quick to look up their meanings. Look first at the whole spread. Are the colors of stones and sephiroth harmonious, or do they clash? Are there clusters of one color? Which colors are missing in the spread? Look for patterns of color and shape. Do the stones fall in their natural places — that is, on the sephiroth with which they are naturally aligned — or are there conflicting aspects? Which stones are missing? Often what is missing is what's most significant. When you have truly grasped the whole, examine each part.

Starting at the top, with Crown, the first sephirah, look at each stone. Hold the stone you've placed on Crown in your hand and try to feel what it says to you. Does the color or shape remind you of anything? Is it pleasant or unpleasant to the eye and hand? Feel the edges and the weight; daydream a little, letting images flow into your mind. This is an important step in interpretation. Those images will provide the flow of psychic energy that links one stone with another and makes a reading significant.

Move next to the second sephirah, Wisdom, and repeat this process with the stone you've placed on it. Continue through the entire Tree, letting each of the stones "talk" to you before you look up their meanings. When you have sensed each stone — especially as you become more familiar with *The Crystal Tree* and the psychic flow — you may not need to look up the meanings. Until then, however, there are brief interpretations of the stones in appendix A and longer, fuller ones in chapter 2. Remember that the interpretation of a stone is greatly influenced by the sephirah where it is placed. Consult the brief list of the sephiroth and their areas of influence in appendix A and the longer section on their meanings found in chapter 4.

There are three levels of meaning listed for every stone. The physical level deals with daily events and ordinary life. The psychological level is more concerned with motivations and personal growth. The spiritual level deals with the progress of the soul. (*The Crystal Tree* is non-denominational; it can be used for purely secular purposes as well as for serious spiritual insight, depending on what the user wants.)

Then there is the Shadow. The Shadow is the negative side of every positive quality, and it should be taken into account, along with the more pleasant side of every interpretation. The Shadow is always there; it's up to you whether to emphasize it or concentrate on the positive side. You won't get rid of the Shadow by ignoring it or repressing it, but by knowing it exists and guarding against it.

The full interpretations in the text and the capsule interpretations in appendix A will help you to understand your readings, but don't rely on them too much. Stones are individualists, and you may find that one stone or another has taken on new meaning to you.

What Kinds of Readings Can You Do?

The Crystal Tree can be used in many ways; the stones and even the Tree of Life are flexible, and you will probably develop some new ways of using them yourself. (If you do, I'd appreciate hearing about them from you; you can write to me care of the publisher.) In general, *The Crystal Tree* can be used for three basic kinds of readings:

> For a situation
> For a character reading
> For past, present, future

The Crystal Tree can also be used in conjunction with other psychic disciplines; please see Part Four.

Situation Readings

The Crystal Tree can help define all the angles and influences of a particular situation, such as a job, a relationship, or a health condition. Because the Tree of Life reveals the situation's effects on all areas of life, it gives a meaning that is deeper than a simple good-bad or yes-no. However, it's up to you to honestly interpret and then weigh all the factors in a situation. *The Crystal Tree* is meant only to guide your thoughts, not to make your choices for you.

When doing a situation reading, you should concentrate on the situation as you choose the stones. After they are all laid out, you should interpret them in the light of the question. Thus, Crown will not be interpreted as your own personality, but as the central question of the situation and its effect on you. Wisdom will not describe your unconscious mind, but the secret motives and goals involved in the situation (and possibly your own unconscious participation in them); and so forth.

Situation readings can change fairly rapidly, as the situation itself changes. Unless something dramatic happens to alter the situation, it's best to ask the same question only once a week at the most; repeated queries tend to lose their meaning, especially when you are not honestly seeking information but trying to test the system.

Character Readings

Character readings can be done for yourself, for others who are present, even occasionally for people who are not present but are in some way linked to the person choosing the stones (though these readings often are marred by wishful thinking).

When doing a character reading, the sephiroth retain their full significance. The stones also are interpreted with their usual meanings. The challenge is to honestly read what's there and blend the meanings of stone and sephirah.

Readings for others who are present can be useful, if one person is far more knowledgeable about *The Crystal Tree* than the others are, but such readings always must be done in a gentle and humble spirit, without mocking or overemphasizing any qualities. Everyone has some stone in Severity, just as everyone has one in Mercy. It's best to be gentle and to draw inferences quietly. If they seem inaccurate, ask what the stone means to the questioner; this can be illuminating indeed, because many people have private interpretations or associations with stones.

Readings for those not present should only be undertaken when the person choosing the stones is already strongly linked to the absent subject — by marriage or other long-term commitment, by blood, by intimate friendship. In addition, such readings should always be taken with a lot of salt. Concentrate on the absent subject while choosing the stones; if you have a letter or a possession that belongs to the subject, you should hold it in one hand while drawing stones with the other. The interpretation should be tentative, not decisive. It is extremely important that *The Crystal Tree* not be used for idle gossip, prying or attempting to pry into the affairs of others, or other wrongdoing. First, it won't work, and second, evil always rebounds on the doers. You can't break spiritual laws with impunity.

How Often Can Readings Be Done?

You can use *The Crystal Tree* to ask as many questions as you want, but the same question (if you're doing a situation reading) should not be asked more than once a week at the outside. A character reading shouldn't be repeated for six weeks or more. (Character readings do change, as you change and grow.) Readings describe things as they are right now and perhaps six to twelve weeks into the future. Only on a birthday or anniversary can you reach in further. Why? Because at those times you're more aware of yourself; the more aware you are, the further you can see.

Part Four

The Crystal Tree and Other
Psychic Arts

4

The Crystal Tree and Other Psychic Arts

Though *The Crystal Tree* is a new way of looking into the self, it draws on a number of ancient traditions. It weaves together ideas and symbols from many sources: the Jewish Kabbala; both Jewish and Greek systems of numerology; traditional and humanistic astrology; and the medieval Christian tarot.

It is not surprising, then, that *The Crystal Tree* is still linked with the other psychic arts. It can be used to illumine insights gleaned from its forerunners, and the other psychic arts can give depth and definitiveness to *The Crystal Tree* readings. Because all the psychic arts are mirrors reflecting the self from various angles, using two at once can give you a three-dimensional image that could not be obtained from even the most complete single-method reading.

6

The Crystal Tree
and the Tarot

Vivid, complex, delicately and intricately structured, the tarot is one of the most popular psychic arts. Each of its seventy-eight cards has a range of up to a dozen meanings, depending on whether the card is reversed or upright, what other cards are near it, and where it falls in a spread. If this sounds complicated, it is; however, it is also a rewarding study for anyone interested in learning the basic skills and disciplines of psychic work. Of the traditional psychic arts, only the mathematical beauties and shifting patterns of astrology come close to tarot's depth and richness of meaning.

The tarot, with its complex symbolic structure (incorporating the four elements, numerology, and astrology), is also intimately connected with the Tree of Life, and thus with *The Crystal Tree*. Because all the psychic arts are related on many levels, it is worth looking into the structure of the tarot, hoping that by examining common assumptions and shared symbolism we shall better understand the tarot and *The Crystal Tree* themselves as well as their relation to each other.

The Major Arcana

The twenty-two cards of the major arcana are the strongest cards of the tarot. They are a progression of symbols that lead the initiate from desire to fulfillment, ignorance to knowledge, and selfish isolation to union with the Universe. Each card expresses the spiritual truth of a certain step along the Path. There are no suits in the major arcana, as there are in the minor arcana; each card stands on its own, but it is also part of a particular and meaningful order, from 0, the Fool, which begins the usual progression but properly fits before and after every card, to 21, the World, which ends the spiral in perfect balance — and then the Fool begins it all again.

The twin themes — the poles — of the major arcana are balance and change. To find balance, you must change; when balance is found, change rapidly alters it. Constantly changing direction and constantly moving upward, swung back in a circle on the central pole of balance/change, the only path possible is a spiral. The feminine manifestation of God is often called a spinner; we, like thread, are spinning ourselves upward on that spindle, the polar opposites united, balance/change. Like shellfish we expand our shells or die; many seashells grow in a spiral pattern, and they are a universal symbol of life and resurrection. Our spiral path is mapped by the major arcana.

The Minor Arcana

The fifty-six cards of the minor arcana deal with more mundane concerns, though all have spiritual meanings as well. These cards are divided into four suits, the ancestors of the four suits in a playing-card deck: the Wands (also known as Rods or Staves), Cups, Swords, and Pentacles (also known as Disks). Each suit has ten numbered cards and four face cards: king, queen, knight, and page. Each suit also corresponds with one of the four elements; see the section below on the four elements and the four suits.

The History of the Tarot

The origins of the tarot itself are somewhat obscure. Claims have been made that it is ancient Egyptian in origin, but the first known deck of tarot cards surfaced in Italy in the late fourteenth century.[1]

Whether the cards are ancient Egyptian, pagan, or Christian, it is clear that the symbols of the major arcana, at least, long predate the first deck of tarot cards. The Wheel of Fortune is prominent in Boethius' *Consolation of Philosophy,* dating from the sixth century A.D.[2] The Tower may refer to the destruction of the Tower of Babel.[3] The culminating card, the World, is a hermaphrodite dancing in a circling wreath — a symbol that curiously resembles the ancient Chinese yin-yang, whose meaning is very similar.[4]

Likewise, the four suits of the minor arcana have ancient meanings. Not only are they connected with the four elements; the symbols of the four suits coincide exactly with the four parts of the Grail treasure. The Chalice itself — the most famous part of the Grail treasure, and usually called the Grail — corresponds with the suit of Cups, of course. But the lesser-known elements of the Grail treasure also match up: Wands with Longinus' spear, which was used to pierce Christ's side; Pentacles with the plate from which Christ ate at the Last Supper; and Swords with the sword with which Peter cut off Malchus' ear in the Garden of Gethsemane, sometimes also identified with a knife or sword that Joseph of Arimathea used to scrape the blood from the dead Christ's wounds.[5] These symbolic identifications give a meaning and depth — almost a terror — to cards usually dismissed as relatively shallow and mundane.

On a more ordinary note, the suits are also symbolic of the four stations of medieval life: Wands as agricultural workers, Pentacles as merchants, Cups as clergy, and Swords as knights and nobility. Interestingly enough, the four castes of Indian society also fit into these classifications.[6]

Since its first appearance, there have been many versions of the tarot. Perhaps the most influential was the Waite/Rider deck, which appeared in 1910.[7] A.E. Waite, who created it, and Pamela Colman Smith, the artist who drew it, were members of the Golden Dawn, a mystical group that also included the poet William Butler Yeats. Not only did the Waite deck mark the revival of serious occultist thought, by men and women of outstanding intellect, it also was influential in the very concrete sense that most subsequent decks have followed its changes in the traditional format.

For the minor arcana, Waite used pictures that incorporated each card's number and suit with a symbolic representation of its meaning. For instance, the four of Wands (a wedding card) shows four wands arranged as a chuppah, the Jewish marriage canopy. The other elements in the card's design also reflect the card's meaning. This innovation makes interpretation far easier for the reader; it aids the querent as well, who can carry away a vivid mental picture of important parts of the reading — something not offered by a plain arrangement of four wands, ten swords, or seven pentacles.

This arrangement has its disadvantages, however. Some readers find the pictures distracting; the pictures also tend to lock in a certain interpretation by their mood, symbols, and coloring. This explains the proliferation of decks in the past few years: each deck has its individual style and its individual connotations, ranging from the richly medieval Stairs of Gold tarot to the cool-toned, modern Aquarian deck.

The other innovation is less harmless: the switching of two major arcana cards. In traditional decks, the eighth card of the major arcana is Justice, the eleventh Strength. In the Waite deck, they are switched, and almost every deck developed since has repeated this change. Waite's explanation for this was that he had "reasons which satisfy myself."[8] It has been suggested that Waite's reason was to put the cards in astrological order: Strength, the obvious card for Leo (it portrays a lion), should come before the Hermit, identified with Virgo.[9] However, I feel strongly that the original order was the correct one and that attempts to force the various psychic arts into exact conformity with one another are bound to fail. There are strong links between them, but no exact equivalencies, and trying to make them all line up neatly seems to indicate a slavery to rationalism and neatness and failure to understand the shifting, metaphorical nature of the symbols we use. Therefore, in this discussion, we return Justice to its original place, after the Chariot and before the Hermit, and put Strength where it is most needed, after the Wheel of Fortune and before the Hanged Man.

The Four Elements

The tarot is structured around the four elements of fire, earth, air, and water. Since every schoolchild knows that there are 103 elements that make up all material things, how can a system that recognizes only four elements apply today?

It does — but you have to leave the realm of chemistry and and move to metaphysics. Chemically speaking, the elements are not elements at all. Confusion arises because the same word is used for both, and the concepts are similar: the basic structures and qualities that are combined to form all imaginable forms. However, in chemistry the elements are physical; in metaphysics, they are spiritual. The four elements are symbolic ways of classifying the energies that, balanced or imbalanced, exist in all of us.

The four elements provide the structure for most of the psychic arts. In astrology, they are manifested in three modes: cardinal, fixed, and mutable. Every sign is a unique combination of one element and one modality. In the tarot, they are symbolized by the four suits. In *The Crystal Tree*, each sephirah belongs to one of the four elements. Understanding the four elements thus becomes extremely important to anyone interested in psychic work.

What are the four elements? The simple answer is fire, earth, air, water. In the descriptions below, we look at the four elements in their purest forms: remember, though, that no person ever

manifests only one element. Even an element that is woefully un-
derrepresented is there; even one that is dominant is tempered
by the presence of the others.[10]

Fire

Fire is symbolized in the tarot as the suit of Wands. In astrology,
the fire signs are Aries, Leo, and Sagittarius. Fire corresponds to
Carl Gustav Jung's intuitive type.[11] Fire rules the sephiroth Crown
and Severity; with water, it rules Foundation.

Fire is the spirit: the life force that drives all things to grow,
flower, reproduce, and die. Though fire can be brilliant, it is by
nature neither stable nor logical; instead, it leaps intuitively. Its
intuition is not sensitivity to others' feelings, but rather an immediate grasp of an entire image, problem, or idea. Restless, seeking,
passionate, fire knows only itself and in the light of its white flame,
all things are revealed as spirit.

Water

Water is symbolized in the tarot as the suit of Cups. In astrology,
the water signs are Cancer, Scorpio, and Pisces. Water corresponds to Jung's feeling type. Water rules the sephiroth Wisdom
and Beauty; with fire, it rules Foundation.

Water is linked with the soul: the gentle force that inspires
us to worship. Feelings are essential to water, and water's intuition
is sensitivity to emotion of all kinds. Fluid, responsive, giving, water is nevertheless both detached and indomitable. It responds,
but its essence is unchanged; it escapes any attempt to destroy it,
but gladly lets itself be captured. Water links us with the past
through memory and with the future through prophecy.

Air

Air is symbolized in the tarot as the suit of Swords. In astrology,
the air signs are Gemini, Libra, and Aquarius. It corresponds to

Jung's thinking type. Air rules the sephiroth Understanding and Victory; with earth, it rules Kingdom.

Air is mind: the logic and intellect that create and spread ideas. The goal of air is to communicate; because the basis of communication is exactitude, air analyzes and dissects. Unlike the passionate fire and the receptive, all-embracing earth, air is detached, rather than self-contained: communication requires more than one person, and so does love. Air is almost as restless as fire but less impulsive, though the two are similar in their endless seeking for knowledge (in the case of air) and experience (in the case of fire). Conversation, the intellectual sharing of thoughts, experiences, sensations, and feelings, is the realm of air, and it is conversation that binds us to each other more surely than any other tie.

Earth

Earth is symbolized in the tarot as the suit of Pentacles. In astrology, the earth signs are Taurus, Virgo, and Capricorn. Earth corresponds to Jung's sensation type. Earth rules the sephiroth Mercy and Splendor; with air, it rules Kingdom.

Earth is related to the flesh and physical things: the embodiment and agent of thought, feeling, and energy. Earth holds and nourishes; what earth builds lasts. It knows by sensing — by direct perception of the world; earth sees and touches and smells and therefore is both sensual and practical. Receptive and stubborn, generous and strong, earth has an instinct not for feelings but of seasons and times. It possesses a sense of myth, because it is rooted in the slow cycles of the Universe.

The Suits, the Sephiroth, and the Four Elements

Fire and Wands

The link between fire and the suit of Wands — also known as Rods or Staves — may seem surprising at first, but a complex interweaving of ideas binds the two. Wands are trees: trees that we burn for warmth and cooking, trees that shape rituals by supplying incense and the fuel for sacrifices. Wood fires protected our ancestors from wild animals and stimulated music and storytelling. The sacred trees of the Druids are linked with their solar deities and the ritual fires at solstice and equinox.

But when a log fire offers heat and light, it is only returning what the sun gave it long ago. Fire is the sun, the light, and the mysterious energy: "the force that through the green fuse drives the flower."[12] God chose the burning bush as an image of His strength when He first spoke to Moses.[13] That image is worth examining, for it shows the total, instantaneous perception that is fire's hallmark. The bush burns and is not consumed: in other words, it is alive, it grows, for energy it burns sugars that it creates from the light of the sun. Moses was seeing with fire-eyes the process that is usually invisible but that goes on daily in every blade of grass, and in us. We, too, burn and are not consumed; we incinerate food, convert sunlight to vitamins, and the steady flame sustains us.

Trees — wands — give us fire only because they have received it from sunlight. They are rooted in earth and fed by water, and they breathe and renew the air. Trees are the only (conventionally) living thing in the four suits. As ancient, long-lived creatures, they move in a different time frame than we do; though perception is instantaneous, the process of growth is slow. This explains the apparent contradiction between the speed and impulsiveness of fire and the slow, steady growth of trees.

Wands are not only living trees, but also the wood that lives even after the tree is cut. Sacred and powerful because their parent tree is sacred and powerful, wands are truly called magic wands, fulfilling a dual purpose: They are both disciplinary rods and staves to support us, as shown in their relationship with the sephiroth they rule.

Crown is fire/wands in their pure aspect, as creator spirits and the basic energy of life. Though the Sun — another attribute of Crown — is not God, it is a symbol of godhead, just as the burning bush was. Crown is that individual spark in each person that the Quakers call the Inner Light. It is the noblest aims, the highest standards, the purest personhood.

Severity is the disciplinary rod aspect of fire/wands. It is the borderland of personality, where everything must be fought for, and it encompasses both the inner demons of fear and emotional scars and the innate limits of our powers. Until you struggle there — with the past, with your fears, with the possibility and ultimately the reality of failure — you will not truly know yourself. Frightened by the dark, you can refuse to try anything new, or you can try many things without sticking to any of them, moving on before you've had a chance to succeed or fail. Both tactics guard against real failure and real growth. Severity teaches you your limits, but it also teaches you your strengths — which are revealed only by struggle and testing.

Foundation will be discussed below.

Water and Cups

Cups contain water; in this case, the symbolism is apparently easy to understand. Yet the mythic resonance of the combination of Cups and water deserves to be explored. Cups is a dual symbol: the created holding the uncreated. On the most literal level, the cup itself — made of wood (Wands) or clay (Pentacles), shaped by an edged tool (Swords) — is an artifact, made by the human hand; the water within is created by God. The symbolic levels endlessly resonate to the same note. The cathedral holds prayer, the flesh holds a soul, the skull holds a mind — all contained in the Universe holding a world, a world holding life. Each created thing holds something it cannot create, something made at a higher level. Art is an attempt to catch and hold the higher level by creating a cup — a song, a poem, an image, a dance — to contain it.

Jesus speaks to the woman at the well of living water — himself — the water in the holy cup; once we drink it, we shall neither thirst nor die.[14] Once again, the Uncreated lives in the created, as a heart beats imprisoned by ribs. The water (and metaphorically, the heart) must be able to get free, to share, or it goes stagnant.

One of water's qualities is that it changes: pulled into tides by the Moon, borne as clouds by the wind, raised as mist from a pond on a sunny spring morning, chilled into temporary stillness as ice or frost. Water carries feelings, which change and flow; the cup is the permanent commitment to love or hate that shapes and contains the water. Change the shape of the cup and the water will re-form.

Wisdom is water's first manifestation in the Tree of Life. Because water flows, because it is subtle and secret in underground streams and hidden wells, it is a symbol of the unconscious mind, which knows a great deal without saying it outright. You have to dowse for insight as you dowse for hidden water. Intuitions trickle into consciousness; the soul and the emotions will not be ruled by logic. Wisdom shows that which is hidden, reveals motives, and uncovers the object of a search. The chief Grail treasure was, after all, the Grail itself: the Chalice.

Beauty is a more physical manifestation than Wisdom. Water finds its own level, and water here seeks balance, harmony, the expansive warmth and affection of undemanding friendship. In its grandest container, the ocean, and its noblest, human veins carrying it as blood, water is both terrifying and beautiful, and its balance is not stagnant stillness but a living, shifting rightness expressed in the flux of tides and pulse. On a practical level, Beauty is not a product of creams and cosmetics, but a natural attribute of balance: between mind and body, between open and hidden waters (what is rightly expressed and what is rightly kept silent), between the cup and its contents.

Foundation will be discussed later.

Air and Swords

Contradiction seems to be the essence of this pair of symbols. We speak of things that are as light as air, while others are heavy as iron. Symbolically, air is detached yet communicative. The apparent paradox is solved by the application of logic — air's basic principle — which cuts away the false assumptions that disguise the relation of air and Swords. They are alike, but alike in unexpected ways.

"Light as air" means 14.7 pounds per square inch, a weight called one atmosphere. A medieval knight on horseback carried a sword that weighed, usually, between two and three pounds — far less than the weight of air we carry daily, hourly. Because air is essentially humankind's element, it is almost invisible to us; we wear it, breathe it, carry it like a crown about us. Air's detachment is not the opposite of communication but its necessary condition: communication by definition requires that there be two or more people participating, therefore that there be physical separation. In a kind of fortunate fall, our lonely isolation has made us poets.

The sword divides, making communication possible in two ways: by allowing us to recognize ourselves as separate persons, and by using logic to analyze. The sword is a weapon and therefore is built to divide, as logic is created to analyze; both weapons and logic seek the opponent's weak spot. Even the English language recognizes this intrinsic similarity: those whose arguments are over-precise *split* hairs and *chop* logic. Moreover, both swords and logic can be used indiscriminately for doing good or evil, for useful or useless work. The sword is unconcerned with what it cuts — necks, underbrush, a loaf of bread are all sliced with knives of one kind or other. The purity of a logical exercise is not altered one bit by the absurdity of its premises; so long as the logic is proper, the conclusion will be logical — though absurd. Iron, the sword-metal, is the traditional enemy of the "little people" (elves and nature spirits in legend; the common people in these days) because logic is the enemy — all too often — of any other way of thinking.

In some ways air and Swords seem inhuman, but actually they are most human. The air is truly our element; we cannot live in fire, water, or earth, though we cannot precisely live without them. Air's sephiroth will bear out this observation.

Understanding, for example, rules primary social and emotional ties: family and friends. It would almost seem to be under water's rule. However, there is more than emotion to relationships. To be shared and understood, emotion must be communicated (as must fire's insight and earth's sensations). Most families love each other most of the time; their troubles often lie in their inability to communicate — to analyze a problem and put it in words another person can understand, or to separate themselves from their situation and see the other person's point of view. Air stands for communication: we speak by shaping the air, and our words travel through air. But just as water's intuition posits a world of secret connections and underground streams, air's communication requires a world where things and people are divided and separate. These are all air functions, and they are beyond doubt as necessary to family relations as the deepest affection and loyalty are. As for friendship — and ultimately erotic love — it is based and fed upon communication; there is no other way two persons can meet and understand one another well enough to spend much time together.

Victory, the seventh sephirah, carries the same seemingly contradictory meanings. This sephirah deals with romantic love, but it also relates to the intellect and the limits of desire. Only the false assumption that logic precludes love — that recognizing separateness destroys any true bonds — can make this pairing seem contradictory. Without limits love dies; marriage demands that you remain faithful to one person, because without that limitation trust would end and with it the marriage. In other words, sometimes structures — limitations — are what shelter the desirable. You can't have everything; if you always choose to keep your options open, you ultimately choose to go nowhere and do nothing.

Kingdom will be discussed later.

Earth and Pentacles

Earth is richly symbolized by Pentacles: by their careful crafting, by their appeal to eye and hand, by their materials (the treasures of the earth, whether fruits or gold). The pentacle design itself is strongly symbolic as well: when the five-pointed star points downward, it symbolizes greed, diabolism, and destruction; when it points upward, it is a symbol of strength in holiness and the proper use of the five senses.

In the tarot card design, the symbol is engraved on a disk, suggesting a plate that is ever replenished. In fact, the Pentacles are not merely under the element earth, they symbolize the Earth itself: called God's footstool[15] and specifically claimed, along with its riches, as a treasured possession of God's.[16] The beauty and abundance of earth and of the Pentacles are blessings from heaven. The Pentacles do not merely stand for worldly things and money; though some tarot decks actually call them Coins, wealth is only an attribute, and not their most important attribute. They are fecund; this suit and element are fruitful and multiply. They love abundance, but it is always earned by hard and careful work.

Mercy, the first earth sephirah, shows the Earth in its role as source of strength and comfort. It is ruled by Venus, a planet associated with more than amorous delights. Venus rules values and responsible love: the twin sources of our greatest strengths. Earth's great stability and solidity give the advantage here.

Splendor, the second earth sephirah, shows the results of all the hard work. It relates to money, children, worklife; it is called Splendor because these things are the glory of our lives on Earth.

Kingdom will be discussed below.

Foundation

Together, fire and water rule the sephirah Foundation, which represents the structure of the spiritual life. A mystic needs neither logic nor sensation — though they help — but must have the fiery qualities of instantaneous insight and complete passion as well as the water qualities of subtle wisdom and intuition.

Kingdom

Together, earth and air rule the sephirah Kingdom. Between sensation and logic, a complete worldly life can be constructed. When Foundation and Kingdom work together, the result is a total life as it was meant to be lived. We are both animal and spiritual beings, and both sides deserve honor and praise; we were designed as we were meant to be, in balance with one another and with ourselves.

The Major Arcana and the Sephiroth

The major arcana are connected with the Tree of Life in two ways. Each card of the major arcana is identified with one of the twenty-two paths that link the sephiroth. (See Figure 6.1.) We are not dealing with the significance of the paths, because they are not used in mundane divination. Each sephirah also is linked with two cards of the major arcana. Since there are twenty-two cards and only ten sephiroth, what happens to the two extra cards?

The first is the Fool, numbered zero. Because the Fool signifies new beginnings, jumping into things, steps on a spiritual journey, the Fool rightly belongs before every sephirah. It takes the Fool's daring — as well as his ignorance — to move on; he never knows where he is going, and no more do we, as we step from one sephirah to another.

The last card, the World, also is not included in the sephiroth, because the World is the whole Tree of Life. The World shows a woman with covered loins dancing in a circling wreath and surrounded by the four creatures that symbolize the gospels (and of course the four elements). The loin covering, however, hides the fact that she is a hermaphrodite: the ultimate symbol of balance. She/he may even be Tiresias, the Greek prophet, who became a woman when he found two snakes coupling: a symbol of the reuniting of all dualities. (Snakes are also considered a symbol of wisdom and renewal when associated with the Tree of Life; they

Figure 6.1 The Twenty-Two Paths of the Tree of Life

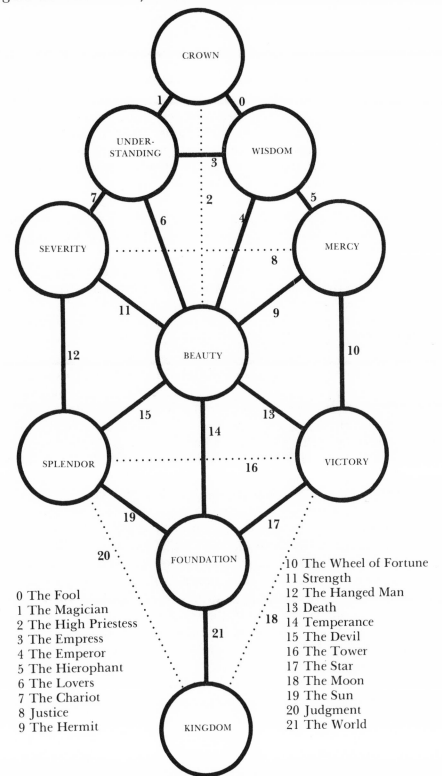

0 The Fool
1 The Magician
2 The High Priestess
3 The Empress
4 The Emperor
5 The Hierophant
6 The Lovers
7 The Chariot
8 Justice
9 The Hermit
10 The Wheel of Fortune
11 Strength
12 The Hanged Man
13 Death
14 Temperance
15 The Devil
16 The Tower
17 The Star
18 The Moon
19 The Sun
20 Judgment
21 The World

symbolize evil only when associated with the Tree of Knowledge.[17]) After seven years as a woman, Tiresias came upon the same snakes coupling again and was returned to manhood.[18]

The World, then, is a card that depicts the reconciliation of opposites (the major theme of the Tree of Life itself, with its emphasis on balance) and of the wisdom gained by that reconciliation. Is it any wonder that this card covers the whole Tree of Life?

The rest of the major arcana cards, numbered one to twenty, are linked with individual sephiroth. (See Figure 6.2.) The major arcana first are divided into two cycles of ten and then taken in order; the first sephirah, Crown, has the first and eleventh cards, the second sephirah has the second and twelfth, and so forth.

Crown: The Magician and Strength

Crown, the pure and burning self, has two manifestations: as the Magician, who creates or takes what he wants, and as Strength, the woman holding the mouth of a lion.

The Magician is a card of power but also of childish notions of controlling the Universe. The Magician is Christopher Marlowe's Dr. Faustus, who sold his soul in return for power and ended by using it to cheat horse-copers (the medieval equivalent of used-car dealers).[19] He is also Peter Beagle's Schmendrick the Magician ("you won't have heard of me"), a mage so incompetent that he "can't turn cream into butter."[20] Though the tragic, eloquent Faustus (who is dragged to hell at the end of the play) and poor, comical Schmendrick may not seem to have much in common besides their profession, neither one understands the order of things. Faustus values power above all else because he wants to be godlike; he does not realize that power doesn't make a god. Faustus can only play monkey-tricks with his power because he himself is only a monkey trying to show off. Though a greater man could have done greater things, a greater man would not have valued power over his soul. Schmendrick's lack of understanding is the cause, not the result, of his incompetence; once he learns and

Figure 6.2 The Major Arcana and the Sephiroth

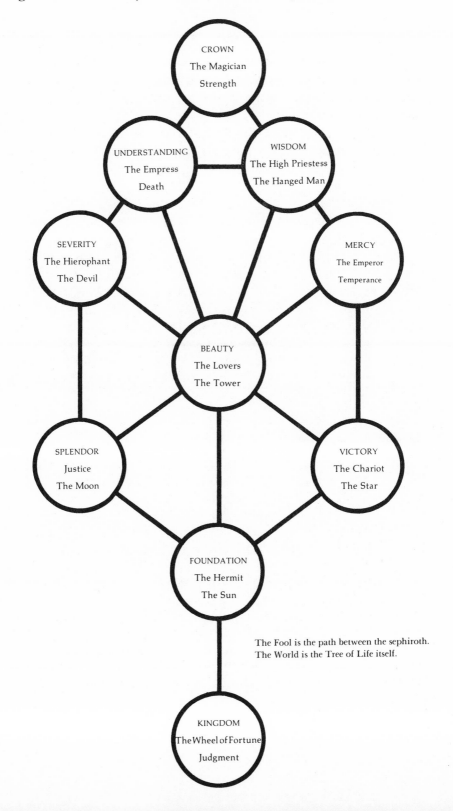

CROWN
The Magician
Strength

UNDERSTANDING
The Empress
Death

WISDOM
The High Priestess
The Hanged Man

SEVERITY
The Hierophant
The Devil

MERCY
The Emperor
Temperance

BEAUTY
The Lovers
The Tower

SPLENDOR
Justice
The Moon

VICTORY
The Chariot
The Star

FOUNDATION
The Hermit
The Sun

The Fool is the path between the sephiroth.
The World is the Tree of Life itself.

KINGDOM
The Wheel of Fortune
Judgment

champions the order of things, his power comes at last under his control.

The Magician, then, represents the self seeking power, and more often than not, seeking the wrong kind of power or seeking it in the wrong ways. Once you learn the order of things (as laid out in the Tree of Life), you achieve power and can use it properly.

Strength is another aspect of the self: the poised, balanced self that already knows the proper priorities. Usually depicted as a woman holding the jaws of a lion, the card is the symbol for internal balance between the physical and spiritual. It also indicates a sense of self that is strong enough to make manipulation and emotional blackmail impossible — the person with Strength will neither submit to them nor impose them on others. Strength is the healthy self that has turned the Faustian quest inside out: instead of seeking power so it can be like God, it seeks godliness — knowing and serving the proper spiritual priorities — and as a result attains power. This power is not wasted on monkey-tricks, but is used for self-control.

Wisdom: The High Priestess and the Hanged Man

Wisdom is easily identified with the High Priestess; the symbolism is clear. The High Priestess is a woman of silence, learning, solitude; indeed, in the Proverbs she is called Wisdom.[21] Her role is like that of Diana, Isis, and all the other virgin goddesses: protector and slayer of the night creatures and wild animals, respository of memory and wisdom. The sephirah Wisdom rules the unconscious, the psychic, and the creative parts of the mind: all the interior, silent places where the High Priestess lives. Everyone needs a *temenos* — a sacred grove, a sheltered place where dark things can come into the light.[22] The High Priestess, in the dark places of the mind, holds memory, weaves new images and ideas, studies the Torah (which is more than the first five books of Moses). From the darkness comes her Wisdom.[23]

The Hanged Man is more problematic. Indeed, it is a difficult card in any context. It is usually interpreted as being of good luck to people who do creative work. The Hanged Man follows his own path and is willing to sacrifice himself for wisdom. Here is the link: the Hanged Man is the dying god who suffers for the sake of wisdom. He is Odin, who hung nine nights on the world tree Yggdrasil in order to win the runes — magic words, the alphabet, poetry — for his people.[24] And Wisdom is poetry and creativity, inner wisdom, a sense of the order of things. The Hanged Man is active where the High Priestess is passive — and neither is better than the other; both have their place in the eternal dance. The Hanged Man does; the High Priestess is. Both are seeking the wordless, mystical sephirah Wisdom.

Understanding: The Empress and Death

Understanding, that warm and communicative sephirah, is naturally connected to the fertile, giving, affectionate Empress. But how can it be linked with Death as well?

The Empress is a woman of power and authority. She represents the family's influence on Understanding. When the family is nurturing and able to share feelings honestly, Understanding is fulfilled — able to play its role. Yet there is a stage for every family, happy and nurturing or violent and destructive, where the children must leave home. Parental authority must end, and the children must become responsible for themselves. Good parents desire this, because it is part of the order of things that children should grow up. (They also grieve a little, but that's natural.) Their aim in raising children is to bring up happy, healthy adults, not to exercise power over other people.

This is where Death comes in. Death is not physical death — *you cannot foretell physical death with either the tarot or The Crystal Tree.* Death is both death and resurrection; the necessary, often painful end of one stage of life and the beginning of another. Leaving home is a death-and- resurrection experience; so are marrying, retiring from a job, and many other physical and spiritual experiences. Death is that necessary separation: a separation we have already seen as essential to communication. There must be some space; the changes Death brings — changes on many levels, changes that can be agonizing — open up new space.

Mercy: The Emperor and Temperance

Mercy's ground is strength and self-respect. The faults we judge most severely in others are those that we most hate in ourselves. We can afford to be merciful where we are strong. This mercy is not a blind eye to wrong, but the willingness to forgive. When the woman was taken in adultery, only the sinless Jesus could both condemn the sin and forgive the sinner. When you feel strong and happy — when your life is in equilibrium and at peace — is the time to start a diet, confront your past, tackle difficult problems. Then you are most ready to forgive yourself and others, and then you are strong enough to face troubles that ordinarily would distress you beyond bearing.

The Emperor symbolizes the kind of self-respect derived from ruling and controlling yourself. Because he is his own master, he is an emperor; worldly wealth and position have nothing to do with his spiritual power. Moreover, because he is in that position of strength he is able to have mercy over others; an emperor has the power to pardon criminals.

Temperance is a less worldly symbol of the self-possession implicit in Mercy. This symbol is the mixing of ingredients in the right proportions. Once again, we're back at the order of things. Here Mercy is expressed as the knowledge of priorities; strength and self-esteem come from an ability to see yourself and others in the proper light. Furthermore, Mercy results in fairness to others and an ability to choose the right thing.

Severity: The Hierophant and the Devil

Severity identifies faults and fears, and it struggles to overcome them. The major arcana cards associated with this sephirah show the two ways of initiating change: The Hierophant leads, the Devil drives.

You can recognize your own faults by observing others who, like the Hierophant, have already learned how to deal with their weaknesses. The Hierophant is an instructor in spiritual matters. The card has an undeserved reputation for self-righteous stuffiness, perhaps because the word hierophant is not in common use, perhaps because it is a specifically religious image and some influential occultists distrust organized religion. (If the card were called the Guru, its role would probably be more easily accepted.) The Hierophant also represents your own standards of conduct; when you compare what you know you should do with what you are actually doing, you can be galvanized into change.

The Devil in the tarot is not Lucifer, also known as Satan. It is a symbol of all the faults, temptations, fears, and guilts that keep us in bondage, whether they are in you or in other people.

In its role as the, so to speak, interior Devil — your unexpressed fears and nightmares, the violence you have suffered, the hidden knowledge of the harm you have done to others — it is compounded of both the wrongs you have done to others and the wrongs that have been done to you. Together these work to destroy your self-esteem, because they are hidden — your deepest secrets — and because you are ashamed of having hurt others and of having been hurt yourself. Ultimately you may come to identify all these hidden horrors as your true self, and you begin to feel as loathsome as your inner secret.

It is called the devil because it chains you with your consent. All of that can be forgiven, has no real power except what you consent to give it, just as Satan has no power over someone who has asked for God's protection. Yet there are times when the inner demon drives you to seek out goodness, to forgive and to ask for forgiveness, to get help to erase the horrors. How? By making you so miserable that the only alternative is to change, to understand and examine the secret, to forgive yourself and others. In that way, the suffering can be turned to good use; later you will be able to help others by drawing on your own painful experiences.

The "exterior" Devil — the faults and sins of the world — can stimulate change by showing you the results of your own faults in someone else. If you have a minor drug habit, seeing someone in the last throes of heroin or cocaine addiction can shock you into giving it up. If you cannot control your temper, a clear sight of the destructiveness of violence — a murder trial, even the sight of someone bruised and bleeding from an enraged attack — can teach you that there are better ways to handle anger.

All this may seem harsh and painful; who wants to deal with faults, or recognize them as being destructive to him/herself and others? But look again at that last paragraph: there are worse things than making the painful effort to change.

Beauty: The Lovers and the Tower

Beauty, the first sephirah of emerging adulthood, is allied with the Lovers card (apparently very appropriate; the first thing most new adults do is fall in love) and the Tower (seemingly less appropriate, with its aura of doom and destruction).

The Lovers is undoubtedly a card of love — falling in love, learning what is important both in love and in a lover — but more a card of making proper choices in all areas of life (making choices is one of Beauty's chief roles). The original design of the Lovers (still used in such decks as the Marseilles Tarot) shows a young man choosing between an older woman and a younger one. This picture has Freudian overtones of choosing between the mother and the lover; in general, it deals with separation from parents as well as the other issues and choices of growing up.

The Tower is a frightening image of lightning striking a high tower; two people are falling from the riven tower. How can this be associated with the overflowing spirits of Beauty? Yet it logically follows from the choice made in the Lovers, for the Tower destroys in order to build. It clears the way for new and more appropriate edifices. In other words, if the Lovers indicates choosing adulthood or childhood, the Tower will carry out that choice: destroying either the bonds of childhood or the hopes of adulthood. This does not suggest that becoming an adult means severing all childhood ties and cutting off communication with your parents, but it does require some opportunity for freedom, some physical and emotional separation from home, and often some healthy anger and rebellion.

Victory: The Chariot and the Star

Victory's ambiguous mix of discipline and desire has been explored at length already; the Star and the Chariot provide the images to fit the roles.

The Chariot is an image of control: The charioteer holds the reins of two sphinxes. The discipline of the Chariot — and of Victory — is the self-control pictured here, for the sphinxes are the charioteer's own body and soul, conscious and unconscious minds, good intentions and selfish temptations. In order to do the creative work ruled by Victory, you must be in control of yourself; in order to have the happy marriage (or other strong commitment) promised by Victory, the partners must each put the commitment above individual needs and desires and work together.

The Star is one of the loveliest cards of the major arcana, lovely both in design and meaning. It signifies strong attachments between people who are not related by blood; just as the constellations, whose power is so manifest in the science of astrology, are connected only by our perceptions of them, so the friendships and passions of the Star are connected only by perceived affinity, perceived goodness: there is no blood tie. That kind of love can only belong to Victory, because it relies on communication, a balance of privacy and sharing, and freedom to express the self.

Love is a kind of gravity: too close, and the swinging orbs crash and die; too far, and they miss one another entirely. At the proper distance, they create a binary star of intense magnitude. Victory expresses that exact distance, the equation of love.

Splendor: Justice and the Moon

Splendor's harvests and rewards are clearly connected with Justice: getting what you deserve. Justice is the most consciously balanced of all the major arcana cards — the figure of Justice actually holds the scales — and it is indeed fair. But it is allied with the mental and material side of life; what governs the fairness of the spirit and soul?

The Moon as a heavenly body is linked with the sephirah Wisdom. The major arcana card called the Moon is linked with the sephirah Splendor. Some of the rewards, then, are not necessarily readily apparent; the Moon is rarely obvious. The Moon "rewards" all the hidden, unforgiven sins and guilts in one way or another: nightmares, neuroses, certain illnesses, for example. This process is not always what brings on illness and suffering, but the Moon — part of ourselves, not an outside force — automatically reacts to hidden shames and sins by trying to remind us of them, so they can be confessed and forgiven. Because the unconscious cannot write us a letter, it can only work as clearly as it can: through conscience (which is often ignored), then through dreams. But how many people really listen to their own dreams? Through all the ways at its disposal, the unconscious tries to remind us that something's wrong, and we try to ignore that uncomfortable situation.

The Moon does more than punish, though. It also rewards: with creativity, with joy, with clearer and clearer dreams as we listen more closely and try to understand, with inspiration, with balance and health. These are not rewards that other people can count — or steal — but they are infinitely satisfying.

Foundation: The Hermit and the Sun

Foundation, the sephirah of spiritual power, has an inward and an outward manifestation. The Hermit goes inward, toward the mountains and deserts of the self, where he/she can learn and grow without distraction. The Sun radiates outward and bathes others in its own pure and nourishing light.

The Hermit represents the soul's need for space, solitude, peace. Only in emptiness is there room to grow; the world is left behind only because it distracts from the contemplation of God.

The Sun is both the source and (in a lesser sense) the result of spiritual strength. It is a metaphor for Divine love and power radiating outward from heaven; the holy rays feed us as actual sunlight feeds plants and trees. After a time as the Hermit — spent drawing in strength and wisdom — the soul returns to act as the Sun does: to feed and help others by the light it sheds.

Kingdom: The Wheel of Fortune and Judgment

Kingdom, the structure and culmination of the created world, is represented by the Wheel of Fortune and by Judgment.

The Wheel of Fortune — the perpetually spinning circle — suggests the world even by its shape and movement. Its meaning is also clear: the changes that come to all of us in turn, the uncertainties and the varying luck that can drastically alter the lot of even the most stable, staid, steady person.

Judgment symbolizes the end of the world, the results and rewards of the way each person has chosen to live, work, think, act, love, and be.

Together, the seemingly random events of the Wheel of Fortune and the strict accountability of Judgment form the structure and order of the Universe, the dance of heaven.

The Tree of Life as a Tarot Spread

The Tree of Life spread, which is the essential structure of *The Crystal Tree,* is often used as a tarot spread. Each individual sephirah has the same meaning, whether cards or stones are used. The Tree of Life can be used with the tarot in several ways: in a brief reading that answers one question, using a single card in each sephirah; in an ordinary reading that covers six to twelve weeks in the future and handles present problems, using three cards in each sephirah; or in a major reading that takes more than an hour to interpret and works with a full year in the future, or a complete current personality reading, using seven cards in each sephirah, along with eight additional cards in what is called a daath pack, laid outside the Tree of Life.

To do a tarot Tree of Life spread, lay a single card at the place of each sephirah. If one of the more complex readings is desired, you should go through the Tree of Life the number of times necessary. Exactly as if you were dealing a poker hand, you must make the rounds each time, placing a card on each sephirah in turn, then repeating the process until three or seven cards lie on each of the sephiroth. With the longest spread, you must have a daath pack; these eight cards are laid down last. A daath pack of five cards is sometimes used with the intermediate spread, but it is not a necessity.

What is a daath pack, and how does it work? Since the Tree of Life is structured and exact, these cards fall outside the realm of order it represents. The daath pack symbolizes forces at work that you're unconscious of, repressed desires and feelings, and ideas and urges that will operate not only in one area of life but over and over again, throughout the Tree of Life. If a particular sephirah is unclear or very complicated, the daath pack can help clarify it.

Using The Crystal Tree with a Tarot Spread

The Crystal Tree can be used with any tarot spread, not just the Tree of Life. You can lay out the stones in the pattern of a tarot spread (see chapter 10), or you can use one to illuminate the other. Because it is difficult to read the tarot for yourself, I am assuming that you will be doing the reading for someone else, a querent.

If the primary reading is a tarot reading, rather than a Crystal Tree reading, first lay out the cards in the chosen pattern. If it's a Tree of Life pattern, you can use the spread that comes with *The Crystal Tree*. Then ask the querent to choose stones, one by one and without looking, just as in an ordinary *The Crystal Tree* reading. Lay a single stone next to each position (not necessarily each card) in the spread. For a Celtic Cross spread, you'll use eleven stones; for a Tree of Life spread — whether you used one card for each position, or three, or seven — you'll use ten stones, perhaps adding one for the daath pack.

Before beginning the interpretation, you should look over the whole spread to see harmonious and inharmonious combinations of cards, and of cards and stones. Then explain each position and its meaning, interpreting either the cards or stone first, whichever feels more comfortable to you. If the querent wants more information or would like to ask a question, you can use cards or stones alone to answer it, or use them together. (The three-stone or three-card methods described later in this chapter are useful here.)

In interpreting the entire spread, you should consider the cards and the stone equals; they interact to produce a single meaning. Usually the stone symbolizes the ongoing meaning of that place in the querent's life. It can also mean ideas not yet put into words, unspoken tendencies or desires, and the urgings of dreams, psychic faculties, and other unconscious forces. The card usually stands for external influences, concrete occurrences, the fulfillment of what the stone predicts.

If the stone and the card have very similar meanings, the querent is on an even keel (even if unhappiness is indicated, it's getting neither worse nor better in that particular position). If they vary widely, look at the general trend of both cards and stones. If they generally match up, this one position may be a source of conflict. If the stones are generally positive and appropriate and the cards are full of changes, the querent may be going through temporary, external troubles but maintaining a strong sense of self. If the cards are serene but the stones indicate difficulties, the querent may be going through painful emotional processes — working through past problems, for example, or preparing for upcoming changes. The querent who has many divergencies but no clear pattern may be under great stress or unable to accept or express many things about him/herself.

The tarot and *The Crystal Tree* can be used together in less formal ways. During a reading with *The Crystal Tree*, one or two stones may be unclear or need further explanation. Sometimes it helps to let the querent shuffle the tarot deck and cut it into three piles. Turn the piles over and the three cards shown will help clarify the stone's meaning. In the same way, a confusing tarot reading can be made clearer by having the querent choose three stones; they help bring the issue into focus. Very often the problem in these situations is that a complex idea or event is being expressed by a single stone or card; more information — that is, more cards or stones to carry the information — almost always gets the message across.

Notes

1. Alfred Douglas, *The Tarot: The Origins, Meanings and Uses of the Cards* (New York: Penguin, 1973), p. 19.

2. Boethius, *The Consolation of Philosophy*, translated by V.E. Watts (Baltimore, MD: Penguin, 1969).

3. Genesis 11:1-9.

4. Chinese philosphy is so extensive and complex that a single reference cannot do it justice. However, see the I Ching — translations abound — and (for practical purposes) Elson M. Haas, *Staying Healthy with the Seasons* (Berkeley, CA: Celestial Arts, 1981).

5. Emma Jung and Marie-Louise von Franz, *The Grail Legend*, translated by Andrea Dykes (Boston: Sigo Press, 1986), p. 84.

6. *Brewer's Dictionary of Phrase and Fable*, revised by Ivor H. Evans (New York: Harper and Row, 1970), pp. 195, 871.

7. Douglas, pp. 122.

8. A. E. Waite, *The Pictorial Key to the Tarot* (New York: Harper and Row, 1971), p. 100.

9. Douglas, p. 122.

10. Classically, air and fire were known as "masculine" because they were active, while water and earth were known as "feminine" because they were receptive. Such classifications are both deceptive (they have no relation to what masculine and feminine really are) and destructive (dividing people into arbitrary categories not only can cause untold pain for those who don't fit, it can stunt and maim those who force themselves to fit). This system is descriptive, not prescriptive, and in any case, as I made clear before, everyone is influenced by all four elements; it is not possible to be born without some of them. Even if one or perhaps two are not dignified in your astrological chart, they do and must appear in the twelve houses of the horoscope. Everyone has all the signs placed somewhere in his or her chart; that's why a full astrological chart is so much more revealing than a bare sun-sign. And in the tarot, it is rare for any reading to turn up cards of one suit only. Though a querent may show up as the appropriate card for his or her age and sun-sign element, it's equally likely that the querent will show up as a different card in different situations, depending on the role played in that situation.

11. All the psychological types are to be found in C.G. Jung, *Psychological Types*, translated by H.G. Baynes, revised by R.F.C. Hull (Princeton, NJ: Princeton University Press, 1971), pp. 330-407.

12. Dylan Thomas, *The Poems of Dylan Thomas* (New York: New Directions, 1971), p. 77.

13. Exodus 3:2-4.

14. John 4:7-14.

15. Isaiah 66:1.

16. Psalms 24:1.

17. J.C. Cooper, *An Illustrated Dictionary of Traditional Symbols* (London: Thames and Hudson, 1978), pp. 146-151.

18. Zeus and Hera asked Tiresias to settle an argument over whether men or women enjoyed sex more; he was struck blind when he said that women do. In recompense for the blindness, he was endowed with the gift of prophecy. Tiresias was the seer who told Oedipus why Thebes was cursed: because a man living there had slain his father and married his mother. Oedipus discovered that he himself had committed that double crime and blinded himself (his mother committed suicide).

19. Christopher Marlowe, *Doctor Faustus*, in *Five Plays*, edited by Havelock Ellis (New York: Hill and Wang, 1966), pp. 179-182.

20. Peter Beagle, *The Last Unicorn* (New York: Ballantine, 1968).

21. Proverbs 8.

22. C.G. Jung, *Analytical Psychology: Its Theory and Practice* (New York: Random House, 1968), pp. 137-138.

23. For a fascinating fictional view of the Torah, see Philip K. Dick, *The Divine Invasion* (New York: Timescape Books, 1981).

24. Barbara G. Walker, *The Woman's Encyclopedia of Myths and Secrets* (New York: Harper and Row, 1983), pp. 733-735.

7

The Crystal Tree and Numerology

Modern numerology is descended from numerology as practiced by the Greeks (such as Pythagoras, famous for the Pythagorean theorem) and from Jewish *gematria*, which is the numerological part of the Kabbala. In both systems, every letter of the alphabet has a numeric value, and each number has a symbolic value. Your name and birthdate supply the basic numerological information about yourself, with many varied and complex kinds of readings possible, using vowels only, consonants only, the number of a times certain numbers come up, and so forth.

The basic numerological table of values is listed below:

1	2	3	4	5	6	7	8	9
A	B	C	D	E	F	G	H	I
J	K	L	M	N	O	P	Q	R
S	T	U	V	W	X	Y	Z	

To find the numerological value of a name, add the number values of each letter; then add the digits of the answer. For example,

L O U I S A M A Y A L C O T T

3 6 3 9 1 1 4 1 7 1 3 3 6 2 2

$$3 + 6 + 3 + 9 + 1 + 1 = 23$$

$$4 + 1 + 7 = 12$$

$$1 + 3 + 3 + 6 + 2 + 2 = 17$$

$$23 + 12 + 17 = 52$$

$$5 + 2 = 7$$

The name number here is Seven, and Louisa May Alcott would look under the section on Seven for the characteristics of her name number. This is the simplest possible name reading. Usually, vowels and consonants are read separately: the numeric value of the vowels deals with the person's emotional life, that of the consonants with the physical or outward life. Moreover, a numerologist would note the abundance of Threes in the name, the lack of Fives and of Eights, as well as the first vowel and many other matters that we can't go into here.[1]

The other basic numerology reading is the birth-number reading; it proceeds by the same principles. Louisa May Alcott was born November 29, 1832. First, you reduce the year to a two-digit number:

$$1 + 8 + 3 + 2 = 14$$

$$11 + 29 + 14 = 54$$

$$5 + 4 = 9$$

Nine, then, is Louisa May Alcott's birth number. (Incidentally, you will find that every numerologist uses slightly different terminology for the various important numbers, but the basic techniques are generally agreed on.)

Numerology is perhaps the easiest psychic technique to learn, though the interpretation is more complex than it appears. The numbers themselves should not be reduced to a single meaning (One: ambition; Seven: psychic); their meaning are much richer — and much less dogmatic — than that. The number meanings given here are the essential core meanings; in different situations they will emphasize different qualities.

The Numbers and the Sephiroth

The meanings of each number and of its corresponding sephirah in the Tree of Life are intertwined. The basic numerological meanings are often expressed as a flat word or two; the addition of a sephirah and of other symbols should express their complexity better.

One: Crown

One is the number of beginnings, will, single-mindedness, ambition, the self. In its single-mindedness, One can be destructive without realizing it; it simply doesn't notice other people's feelings unless they can be of advantage to itself. One is determined, hardworking, and tireless. On a deeper level, however, One is intensely mystical: the Lord is One, the root of the word Universe is one, One is the essence of all things, the sun and center.

The symbol for One is suggested by its shape. It looks like a spaceship: clean lines and a single purpose, probing the Universe but not necessarily well adapted for returning home. (By the time an ordinary rocket returns, all that's left is the triangular cone — a shape discussed under the number Three.)

In its determination and unawareness of others, One is like the element fire. In its role as the beginning and the begetter, One is related to the sephirah Crown: the pure essence of self, flaming and untamed individuality.

Like all the odd numbers, One is traditionally considered "masculine": that is, active rather than receptive.

Two: Wisdom

Two is the number of balance, giving, and the unconscious. In its search for balance and harmony, Two may give too much or too little, becoming either weak or intransigent. Two is the first number that offers a choice, and many of our words of choosing — alternatives, dilemma — really mean a choice between two things. In some older numerological systems, Two was the number of woman and evil; this evident sexism had its roots in the definition of women as other.[2]

Part of the fear is also fear of night, dreams, psychic powers, and women's mysterious cycles. These are all associated with the Moon, and the curve of the numeral Two is modeled on the waxing crescent of the Moon,[3] which is the two-horned symbol for the number Two. Many people still are terrified of the unconscious, psychic, classically "feminine" part of life; others recognize that we all are androgynous, that men carry an Anima (an internal, female self) and women an Animus (an internal, male self) throughout life.[4]

In its search for balance and its changes, Two is like the element water. In its (sometimes sinister) wisdom, the ancient intuition and the often frightening inner self, Two is linked with the sephirah Wisdom: the search, the searched-for, and the reason for searching, all at once.

Three: Understanding

Three is a sacred number: the number of the Trinity, of the soul, of giving. Medieval Welsh poets expressed their wisdom in triads; Three signifies communication and (through communication) love, emotional ties, and family relationships. Three's openness to new relationships may make it shallow and disloyal. Or, it may become so wrapped up in primary relationships that it regards all strangers with distrust and dislike.

The symbol of the Three is the triangle: like the nose cone of that spaceship, it is ideally fitted for getting home, being adapted to the atmosphere and ready to float. (The space shuttles, too, look less like a rocket than like a triangle.) Three gives us past, present, and future, and the ability to move through the past and present by using memory.

In its desire for communication with others, Three is like the element air. In its loving and sociable aspects, it is like the sephirah Understanding. (A distinction may be useful here. Wisdom is an inner and instinctive knowledge, often not expressed or expressible in words; Understanding is reached only through communication and must be expressible in words or by other rational means.) Talk — conversation — is one of the greatest of family ties. One of the earliest duties of parents is to teach their children to talk. Parents may not be aware that their every action is also teaching the children what and how to communicate: whether to shout or repress or reasonably express emotions, whether physical communication is acceptable or taboo, whether lies or truth are more important.

Four: Mercy

Four is the number of natural stability and strength; linked with the cycle of the seasons, the four cardinal directions, the four elements, all the fourfold symbols. It symbolizes a quiet sensitivity to universal rhythms that sometimes produces a slow psychic intuition, an unnoticed trickle of knowledge from the wind and the rain. Another quality of Four is its unmatched endurance — not only stoic endurance of pain and suffering, but also the quiet stamina of a born hard worker. Like all the numbers, Four has the faults of its virtues: it can be too stubborn, slow-thinking, and materialistic.

The geometric symbol of Four is the square, which perfectly embodies both the number's stubbornness (you cannot roll a square, you must lift and carry it) and its strength (most houses and furniture are based on squares and rectangles, four legs and four walls). In its links to the natural world, its slow responsiveness to the seasons, and its stubborn endurance, Four is like the element earth. Because it is the root and source of strength, it is like the sephirah Mercy, in which you forgive both yourself and others.

Five: Severity

Five is the number of humanity — and therefore of change, risk, sexuality, and excitement. Five is passionate, blunt, uncompromising, vigorous. Five is a crusader and a creator. It jumps to conclusions (and is frequently right, being intensely insightful). Heedless, daring, lively, and social, Five is never bored or boring. However, its endless quest for the new and the exciting can become dangerous and destructive, while its intense and joyful sexuality can become jaded promiscuity.

The symbol for Five is the human body itself. We have five fingers on each hand and five traditional senses; even the shape of our bodies is fivefold, with two arms, two legs, one head. The five-pointed star or pentacle alters its meaning, depending on whether it points up or down; our bodies are five-pointed stars themselves and can point towards our own salvation or destruction.

In its eagerness for new experience, its dramatic sense, and its speed of thought, Five is like the element fire. In its courage, daring, uncompromising toughness and honesty, and willingness to change, Five is like the sephirah Severity. On the surface they seem very different: the lively and daring opposed to the restrictive and repressive. Like most apparent paradoxes, this one is based on false assumptions. Severity is the twin of Mercy: they are the two poles of a single concept. Mercy knows our strengths and offers forgiveness; Severity knows our weakness and offers the impetus to struggle and change our lives. Therefore, Severity needs energy, daring, clear-sighted bluntness: the qualities of Five.

Six: Beauty

Six is the number of responsible love, multiplying the number Two's instinctive wisdom and desire for harmony by Three's communication and social nature — or adding the stability and strength of Four to the search for balance and harmony so characteristic of Two. Either way you add it up, this number symbolizes home and family, commitment, sharing, compassion.

Six is sensitive to beauty, but its ideal of beauty is based not on fashion but on health and balance. Six gives the blessings of completeness, offering complete love: physical passion, emotional sharing, rational commitment. However, even Six has its faults. It can be possessive, sometimes has an over-critical spirit (trying to perfect the loved one), and occasionally refuses to try real life because it will never match the delights of a fantasized existence.

The symbol of Six is variously known as the Shield of David, the Star of David, or Solomon's Seal: the familiar six-pointed star that entwines two triangles. Besides being the most easily recognized symbol of Judaism, it is the pictorial symbol of that multiplication of Three by Two as mentioned before.

In its dependence on feeling, Six is like the element water. In its desire for balance and beauty, it is like the sephirah Beauty. Beauty, the sephirah, is the result of the forgiveness tendered by Mercy and the changes begun by Severity. Beauty is, primarily, balance and blessing, a joyful awareness of yourself as a whole person, healthy in the flesh and happy in the spirit. In some ways, Beauty is the pivot on which the whole Tree of Life swings: the soul progressing through the sephiroth reaches adulthood here at Beauty. Only when the soul has begun to accept and forgive itself — and to change destructive habits and ideas into constructive ones — is the soul truly in balance and ready for the responsibilities of the last four sephiroth.

Seven: Victory

Seven is the number of solitude, books, art, the psychic, and thought. It is a sacred number: there are seven days in the week, seven virtues (also seven deadly sins), seven gifts of the spirit. The Hebrew word "to swear" can be translated literally as "to come under the influence of seven things."[5] Being a prime number, Seven values its individuality, but it seeks always to share its individuality through art, poetry, literature, music. Sometimes the individuality stretches to eccentricity, the need for privacy becomes a mania, and the sacred is caricatured into the profane.

Seven is an ambiguous number, dealing both with limits and the restless yearning to stretch beyond them, demanding privacy and solitude yet using them to reach toward others through art and toward God through mysticism.

There are three symbolic representations of Seven: The menorah, the Jewish ritual candlestick, symbolizes the presence of God;[6] Apollo's seven-stringed lyre symbolizes reason, thought, and logic; and, synthesizing the two, the sonnet, the poem of fourteen lines — twice seven — with its strict rules of rhyme and meter, is the rational, logical, Appollonian vehicle to express both divine and human love. Seven has a Classical form that may be deceptive; its content is Romantic.

With its love of solitude and study and its need to express itself, Seven is like the element air. With its interweaving of desire and discipline, it is like the sephirah Victory. Victory deals with both intellect and mature erotic love — usually considered opposites by those who believe the stereotype of the icy intellectual. However, the basis for a happy married life (or for any other serious emotional relationship) is more than affection and sexual compatibility, important as they are. Marriage requires commitment and communication, both of which fall under Victory. And if a marriage is to last, both partners must have privacy and personal space. Infatuation demands constant togetherness; mature love recognizes the need for some separateness. This is the wisdom of air: that communication requires separateness. The wisdom of Seven is that individuality nourished in silence and space form the matrix of true love and togetherness.

Eight: Splendor

Eight is the number of abundance and material success. It is the first cube: 2 x 2 x 2 = 8. Since it is Four added to itself, it doubles Four's solidity and strength — and sometimes Four's tendency to materialism as well. Four sows the seed; Eight gathers the harvest, saves the increase, and hoards the seed for next year's sowing. Eight deals with all increase: children, money, crops, practical inventions.

The symbol of Eight is the beatitudes, which bestow blessings on the virtuous. The beatitudes continue the theme of harvest and good results: each virtue mentioned is specifically rewarded.[7] Yet these don't promise riches, ease, lottery winnings, power, or status — at least, not in any earthly sense. Though Eight does handle financial and social increase, its highest purpose is to encourage and reward stewardship: that caring for the Lord's gifts, whether they be gifts of virtue or talent or money or the great gift of the Earth itself. From the first we were told to be fruitful and multiply and replenish the Earth; Eight enforces and rewards that command.

In its harvesting and its concern with the material as well as the spiritual, Eight is like the element earth. In the same ways, it is like the sephirah Splendor. Splendor represents the harvest, the rewards of joyous work and craftsmanship, the children of the marriage described in Victory. In some ways it is the most easily understood sephirah in the Tree of Life. The abundance, the rewards, are so clearly material that they employ no paradoxes or high-flown mystical metaphors. Yet is it so clear? The abundance here is not necessarily expressed as the trappings of wealth and ease. Sometimes the abundance and the harvest are purely spiritual: the fruits of the Spirit.[8] Sometimes what is reaped here is not virtue and joy. "Whatsoever a man soweth, that shall he also reap." And "If you sow the wind, ye shall reap the whirlwind."[9]

Nine: Foundation

Nine is the number of completion. Three times three, the triple triad, intensifies the wisdom and holiness of Nine. Nine muses complete the arts; there are nine orders of angels; nine months make a normal pregnancy, time for the child to complete itself in the womb; wonders last nine days. Nine seeks always to close the circle and make everything clear, clean, ready. In excess, this drive for perfection can destroy what is being perfected. Sometimes Nine, knowing that perfection is impossible, attempts nothing instead.

The symbol for Nine comes from Norse mythology. Odin, chief of the gods, hung for nine nights on Yggdrasil, the World Tree, in order to obtain wisdom for humanity.[10] If you can reach completion, stay on your particular Yggdrasil until you break through to wisdom, then you will have attained Nine.

Nine, being a spiritual and emotional number, is like fire and water. Because it endlessly seeks to complete the circle, it is both beginning and end, for circles have neither beginning nor end. Thus Nine is like the sephirah Foundation, which is the spiritual basis for the Tree of Life; we come from God and go to God. Foundation deals with the spiritual and the highest level of psychic and creative work, because they are done with a combination of unconscious wisdom and leaping intuition, of feeling and passion.

Ten: Kingdom

Ten, in ordinary numerology, is reduced to its root number of One. However, even the larger numbers carry their own meanings (expanding on the root meaning), and for the Tree of Life it is best to consider Ten as a separate number: the culmination. Nine was completion in a spiritual sense; Ten is completion in a physical sense. In the act that completes one spiral or cycle, the new one is begun.

The *tetraktys* (1 + 2 + 3 + 4 = 10) expresses the completeness and order of the Universe: one is a point, two a line, three a plane, four a solid, and together they form what is beyond: completion, the law of the Universe.[11]

The symbol for the number Ten is David's "instrument of ten strings."[12] That instrument is the human being: two hands to serve, two feet to walk wherever needed, two eyes to see the glories of creation, two ears to hear God's praise, one mouth to tell others of the goodness of the world, and one heart that must be wholly dedicated.

In its earthly and structural aspects, Ten is like the elements air and earth. For the same reasons, it is like the sephirah Kingdom. Kingdom is the physical source and end of all, just as Foundation is the spiritual alpha and omega. Some materialists mock the mystical, and some who call themselves mystics despise the earthly and physical aspects of creation. Yet God looked on the Universe and the earth and called them good; we can do no less. The world and the flesh too often are lumped with the devil. There is a distinction between the world — the created earth, full of good things and designed as an infinitely fascinating, infinitely instructive parable of God's love — and worldliness, which is a rejection of the spiritual, masking itself as jaded sophistication, scorning ancient truths and fresh insights, sneering at faith and passion, and caring only for status, power, and money. Likewise, there is a difference between the rightful pleasures of the flesh — from a walk on a lovely day to good food to well-expressed sexuality — and the pitiful, desperate pursuit of oblivion through drugs, sex, even jogging, and other addictive behaviors. All these come under Kingdom. It is your choice between the world and worldliness, the flesh and addictiveness.

Using The Crystal Tree
with a Numerology Reading

There are two ways to combine *The Crystal Tree* and numerology. First, you can have a full numerology reading done (or do one yourself) and then compare your numbers with their sephiroth. This approach gives you an idea of the deeper meaning of the numbers and of their place in the order of the Universe; too often numbers are treated in isolation in a numerology reading. In addition, you can check the numbers that are missing from your numerology reading and find their places on the Tree of Life as well. In some ways, what is missing in a numerology reading is as significant as what is most prominent.

Second, you can clarify a numerology reading by drawing three stones for each number. The stones will indicate how that quality or trait is functioning in your current life. Begin by interpreting the stones as they stand on their own and as they apply to the number for which they were drawn. It is especially illuminating, once the first interpretation is done, to place the stones in the sephirah ruled by that particular number and to interpret how they work there. For example, if you're drawing three stones to interpret your name number, and your name number is Seven, you should interpret the stones in the Victory sephirah. Go through the whole interpretive process, noting colors, shapes, clarity, meanings. Look beyond the first three meanings to the Shadow. Check the relations of the sephirah with numbers, with ast, with the four elements, and in the total context of *The Crystal Tree.*

Notes

1. For basic guides to numerology, see the Numerology section of Further Reading.

2. For some interesting reflections on women's roles in society and the meaning of the Moon, see Donna Cunningham, *Being a Lunar Type in a Solar World* (York Beach, ME: Samuel Weiser, 1982).

3. Donna Cunningham, *An Astrologer's Guide to Self-Awareness* (Reno, NV: CRCS, 1978), p. 28.

4. M. Esther Harding, *Woman's Mysteries: Ancient and Modern* (New York: Bantam, 1973), pp. 81-82.

5. *Brewer's Dictionary of Phrase and Fable*, revised by Ivor H. Evans (New York: Harper and Row, 1970), p. 984.

6. J.C. Cooper, *An Illustrated Encyclopaedia of Traditional Symbols* (London: Thames and Hudson, 1978), p. 28.

7. Matthew 5: 3-10.

8. Galatians 5:22-23.

9. Galatians 6:7-8; Hosea 8:7.

10. Barbara G. Walker, *The Woman's Encyclopedia of Myths and Secrets* (New York: Harper and Row, 1983), pp. 733-735.

11. Cooper, p. 119.

12. Psalms 33:2.

8

The Crystal Tree
and Astrology

The Crystal Tree and astrology are linked in two ways: by the planets, which rule both the sephiroth and astrological signs, and by the four elements, which are part of the innate structure of both. The elements were considered in detail in chapter 6, but the complex relation of planets and sephiroth will be examined here.

The Planets and the Sephiroth

Crown: The Sun

Crown signifies the self, pure energy, and the individual spirit. Its ruling planet is the Sun, which is quite literally the parent of the other planets. As the bright center of the solar system, the Sun supplies the energy for all life on Earth. It feeds us and warms us. By day it gives the light by which we see, and at night its light is reflected by the Moon. Its pure energy, its face too bright to look at, is like the flame of the spirit that Crown represents.

Wisdom: The Moon

Wisdom symbolizes the unconscious self, the night side that knows but does not speak directly: only through dreams, poetry, instinct, symbol. Because the Moon's light is reflected, some call it deceptive. Instead, they should see how clean and clear a mirror must be to send back a true image, and thank the Moon for interpreting the Sun's rays in ways we can understand. You can look the Moon full in the face and not be blinded, because its light is indirect, just as you can look at Wisdom full in the face, because it presents the truth symbolically.

Understanding: Mercury

Understanding rules relationships built by communication; no planet deals with communication as Mercury does. Swift-moving and always close to the Sun, its fount of reason, Mercury is the messenger that darts between us. Mercury is less interested in content than in form. Like a telephone wire, it carries all kinds of messages, not discriminating between truth and lies, business and passion. Since Understanding deals with family relationships as well as friendships and love, Mercury's willingness to carry anything becomes extraordinarily important. One of the messages that it can carry is that some messages are forbidden, some words may not be spoken, some stories may never be told. If you learn as a child that certain kinds of messages are not acceptable in your family, you will have a hard time learning to express those messages later on.

Mercy: Venus

Mercy is the root of strength, Venus the fount of passion: how do they fit together? Venus is far more than just a good-luck charm for Lotharios. It has been confined to a sexual place in the Universe by the same sexist thinking that calls the Moon deceptive or evil: since they are considered feminine, they must be either whores (if specifically sexual) or neurotic crones (if not specifically sexual). Venus, the lesser benefic to traditional astrology (Jupiter is known as the greater benefic), provides more than romance. It rules love and self-esteem, compassion and values. It expresses the love described in I Corinthians 13 and in the Christ's words, "Love your neighbor as yourself." To follow that rule, you must love yourself as well as your neighbor, and that is where Mercy comes in. Mercy offers free forgiveness for ourselves and others; its strength is the strength of gentleness.

Severity: Mars

The violence usually associated with Mars is an unjust reputation based on sexual stereotyping. Though war comes under Mars, so does any kind of action, aggression, or moving forward. The link between Severity and Mars is the link between the recognition of the need for change and the forces of change themselves. Severity demands that destructive habits be changed; Mars provides the energy to make that change. Although Severity sometimes attacks external problems (resulting in the great crusades against problems as diverse as drunk driving and taxation without representation), it works most effectively on an internal level: changing yourself. Repercussions vary, from easing a difficult family situation to changing (or trying to change) the world. Where Severity works least effectively is in attempting to change others' behavior without changing your own.

Beauty: Jupiter

Beauty here is the beauty of balance, of physical and emotional health, of everything in its right place. Jupiter, called the greater benefic, rules this sephirah because it is the first sephirah of adulthood (though we move constantly through the Tree of Life throughout life, and are probably working in three different sephiroth at different levels at any one time). Jupiter, the planet of expansion, functions as a kind of secondary Sun; it is the only planet that gives off its own light in addition to reflecting the Sun's. Both Beauty and Jupiter act as gateways: Beauty is the gate the second, external half of the Tree of Life, Jupiter to the outer planets. Jupiter is like a phrase repeated in music, not in its original form, but similar enough to remind the listener of the original theme, the Sun. Beauty is a reprise of the self found in Crown, but now the self has learned the lessons of the first five sephiroth.

Victory: Saturn

Victory weaves desire and discipline into a complex form. It understands the proper relations of things: the right distance to remain from the beloved, the right way to express a feeling, the right form for a poem or play. Saturn guards time and therefore priorities, and Victory understands both. Indeed, one of Victory's activities, the creation of art, is dependent on Saturn's time. Music, poetry, and dance draw directly on time and meter; literature, painting, architecture, and the other arts rely on a subtler sense of rhythm and proportion in both the details and the grand design of their structures.

Splendor: Uranus

Splendor rules harvest, rewards, children, inventions, work, money, and all other forms of increase. Uranus, with its reputation for unreliability, may seem inappropriate in this context, but Uranus rules the new, and all increase is new. Moreover, Splendor usually has unexpected repercussions as well, doubly linking it to Uranus. No child ever turns out the way the parents expect; no successful invention, from the printing press to the paper bag, performs in a vacuum, but brings along with it unforeseen changes in society, work, and ideas. Splendor's reaping may find some strange fruit among the grain. It's a law of nature: you can never do only one thing.

Foundation: Neptune

Foundation is the spiritual beginning and end of us all. Neptune is an unpredictable planet linked with mysteries, psychic influences, and symbols taken for reality. Both fire and water have influence here as well, fire contributing its instantaneous grasp of ideas and its passion, water contributing its instinctive knowledge and its emotional content. In other words, Foundation and its ruling planet can be understood with the soul and spirit (sometimes collectively known as the heart), but they slip through rational thought processes and cannot be nailed down (an earthy attribute if there ever was one). Instead, feel Foundation and Neptune as water does, surrender to them in a fiery ecstasy. Music, art, poetry, prayers, landscapes, dreams — and yes, the gemstones — all can capture the fugitive glory of Foundation, if you are ready for that transcendence.

Kingdom: Pluto

Kingdom is the source and end of all physical creation, and Pluto — that dark, faraway, erratic planet — properly rules it. Here Pluto, king of the underworld (not of hell in any Christian sense, but of the world where the dead were wandering shadows), is guardian of the created Universe, of earthy practicality and airy logic. This sephirah is almost too concrete for metaphors, as Foundation could be nothing but metaphors, but there is a glory in this as well, the common glory of good bread, a well-made garden, a solidly constructed house or mathematical proof, an elegant computer program, a good tool. Ultimately, the physical Universe nourishes us all; there is as much honor in that as in the ecstasies of mysticism. We come from this and we shall return to this, and there is joy in that as well.

Using The Crystal Tree with Your Astrology Chart

In order to compare *The Crystal Tree* with your horoscope (be it a natal, progressed, a Davison relationship chart, or whatever), you must have an accurate horoscope. Knowing your Sun sign or Moon sign only will not be of much help. Though you can cast a chart yourself, using an ephemeris and a good astrology book, it's usually more trouble than it's worth; the ephemeris alone may cost what you would pay a professional chart service for a computerized horoscope with interpretation, list of aspects, and so forth.

When you have an accurate chart, turn to the workbook pages in the back of this book. On the first page, you'll find the Tree of Life especially adapted for your horoscope chart. In the Crown sephirah, write down your Sun sign; in Wisdom, your Moon sign; and so forth. (Each sephirah is labelled with the planet to be placed there.) There are blanks at the bottom of the page to record the exact position of each planet. Let's say you have the Sun in Sagittarius. Write Sagittarius in the Crown sephirah and on the Sun-sign blank record Sagittarius 23°26' (or whatever the exact position is). The Moon in Libra would be likewise recorded in the Wisdom sephirah, and its precise position would be placed on the proper blank. In a very few minutes, you'll be recording Pluto in Leo in the Kingdom sephirah and writing down its position in the blank, and you'll be done.

The results may seem startling. No matter how familiar you are with your own horoscope, this way of looking at it seems to reveal new connections or progressions. Comparing the positions of your planets with the nature of the sephiroth they rule can help clarify how the planets work in your life. Moreover, the Tree of Life will be clearer and more personal for you when you understand which signs — for you — are actually influencing each sephirah.

One important role of the astrological Tree of Life is to show hidden connections between sephiroth. If you have two planets in the same sign, the two sephiroth will be linked in unexpected ways.

For example, a woman — call her Joanna — who has both the Sun and Saturn in Sagittarius will have Sagittarius influencing the sephiroth Crown and Victory. In astrology, the conjunction of the two planets denotes serious intensity of purpose and a need for self-expression[1] or sometimes a dominant, repressive father.[2] (Of course, the two planets can be in the same sign but not be conjunct.) Their conjunction in Sagittarius will tend to repress Joanna's Sagittarian high spirits and (temporarily) tame her urge to wander.

Looking at this combination in the light of the Tree of Life, Victory and Crown will strongly influence one another. Part of Joanna's self-image (Crown) will be from Victory: pride in her self-discipline, strong identification with her creative and intellectual work. Crown will also influence Victory: Joanna will put her whole heart and self into a love relationship, and every word she says must live up to her self-image. Given the natural Sagittarian sense of fair play, we can infer that Joanna not only will be faithful once she's made a commitment, but that she won't make a commitment until she's sure she can keep it forever. Love is too important to Joanna to make a game of it; she'll recover slowly from a bad love affair, and she will never forgive a lie.

Having planets in the same sign is not the only link between sephiroth. Signs belonging to the same element (fire, water, earth, air) will have a slight influence on one another; signs in square (90 degrees apart) or opposition (180 degrees apart) can frustrate one another, while signs in trine (120 degrees apart) or sextile (60 degrees apart) can help one another. If two or more sephiroth in a row belong to sequential astrological signs (e.g., Mercy, Severity, and Beauty belonging to Taurus, Gemini, and Cancer), the relationship between them is heightened and they become much more important.

For example, a man with Mercy in Taurus would find his greatest strengths in his earthy, loving nature and his bulldog determination. With Severity in Gemini, he would tend to talk aggressively, but perhaps have problems expressing the tender emotions that are his strengths. Since Mercy and Severity together indicate the way positive change and growth will come, he should try talking in private with those he loves or perhaps consider the "talking cure" of psychotherapy. When he reaches balance in Beauty, that sephirah is influenced by Cancer: a happier home life and the knowledge of his own tender feelings under his tough shell.

You can use your astrological Tree of Life to enrich your personal readings. Choose and lay out the stones just as you would with the ordinary Tree of Life spread. When you are interpreting, keep in mind the primary quality of the sephirah — Crown's pure selfhood, for example — but also interpret the stone in the light of which sign lies there. This kind of interpretation, incorporating so many factors, is easier to do when you're thoroughly familiar with *The Crystal Tree;* it also helps to be conversant with astrology. Remember that each sephirah represents an area of life under consideration. The corresponding astrological sign indicates your basic attitude toward that part of life or the way it ordinarily functions for you; the stone reveals new developments, challenges, changes, and events in that area.

The astrological Tree of Life, however, lacks the ascendant — a weakness that may be a strength, for those people who do not know their precise birthtimes. There is another way to use astrology with *The Crystal Tree* that includes the ascendant and the twelve houses. This method is given in detail in chapter 10.

Notes

1. Alan Oken, *The Horoscope, The Road and Its Travelers* (New York: Bantam, 1974), pp. 221-222.

2. Betty Lundsted, *Astrological Insights into Personality* (San Diego, CA: Astro Computing Services, 1980), pp. 128-130.

Part Five

Adding Stones and Spreads

9

Choosing New Stones

The stones included with *The Crystal Tree* are carefully chosen according to their meanings, colors, and textures. Yet you may find yourself eyeing a bright stone in a rock shop or wanting to add a rough piece of pumice to your group. Is it possible to add stones to the existing collection?

Yes, but you must be careful. There is a balance in the collection as it stands, and you should try to maintain that balance.

First and most important, wait until you're thoroughly familiar with *The Crystal Tree* before you add any stones. Using *The Crystal Tree* involves more than looking up the meanings of sephiroth and stones. It's like being the leader of a jazz improvisation band — you have to get to know the players and their instruments before you can make any music, and you don't add new players until you're sure of the core group. Until you have a strong, intuitive grasp of the stones included with *The Crystal Tree*, new stones will tend to confuse your interpretations. Get to know each stone's individual psychic presence, learn the ten sephiroth, and you'll be ready to add the stones that will make your version of *The Crystal Tree* unique and irreplaceable.

When you are ready to add stones, you should follow these guidelines.

*Choose stones that are approximately the same size as those
already in the kit.*

A very large stone can be obtrusive and even damage the other
stones; a very small stone can get lost or crushed. Select stones that
are between roughly one-half inch long to one-and-a-half inches
long. Stones should be reasonably thick; a thin, flat stone can be
broken easily by larger stones.

Choose stones in a variety of colors.

Maybe you're enchanted with the intense blues of sodalite and
lapis lazuli or the deep orange-red of jasper. But if you overload
The Crystal Tree with stones of one color family, you'll tip it out
of balance. Too many clear or white stones make the Tree un-
worldly; too many red stones blind it with emotion. Incidentally,
you can tell a lot about yourself by which stones most appeal to
you! See the section on Color Symbolism in chapter 3 for more
details.

Choose stones with a variey of degrees of opacity.

Crystalline stones — whether quartz, amethyst, or even halite
(which, if you lick it, is immediately identifiable as salt) — tend
to have spiritual and psychic meanings. The more opaque a stone,
the more it deals with daily life and emotions, and the less with
spiritual and psychic matters. The distinction is similar to the difference between the minor arcana (opaque) and the major arcana
(crystalline) in the tarot.

Choose stones with a variety of textures.

By all means add some rough stones. Faceted stones can be added,
too, though they will probably be smaller than the other stones
(they're more expensive!). Rough stones are stones in their natural

state; they tend to symbolize raw emotions and ideas in their native context. Polished stones are more abstract and less involved with their surroundings. Though rough and polished carnelian, for example, both deal with friendship, love, and fun, the rough stone would emphasize simple pleasures and wordless, instinctive affinities; the polished stone adds a sense of social relationships, civilities, and intellectual friendships. Faceted stones (or those rounded into cabochon shapes) are a step beyond; these have been cut to show off their best lights, and they are art — shaped to give a sense of structure and beauty. That shaping can come across as artificiality or as loving craftsmanship and care for an important quality.

Before you add any stone to The Crystal Tree, handle it.

Whether it's a polished agate, a chunk of pumice, or a faceted smoky quartz, a stone should feel right in your hand. A stone that gives you a strong, immediate negative feeling is not right for you.

Add no more than three stones at a time, and don't add more until you're completely used to the new stones.

It takes time for you to adjust to the new balance of energies when there are new stones in the group — and it takes time for the stones to adjust to each other. In this, *The Crystal Tree* is like a musical instrument: a piano, which is made up of many separate parts, sounds tinny and plastic when it's new; once the parts have adjusted to one another, the sound is well-seasoned, rich, and harmonious. The separate parts have become a whole.

The one exception to this rule is the process of "doubling" your stones: adding a new set of eighteen stones to the originals. Doubling works well because the stones being added are already in balance with each other and with the original set. You double your stones in order to increase the depth of your readings.

If aventurine, for example, shows up twice in a single reading, it reveals the hidden connections between the two sephiroth where it was placed. It also shows their connections with the sephi-rah Beauty, which is the sephirah linked with aventurine. If you keep a record of your readings, you can watch for stones that often show up twice in a reading. These stones, along with those that you never see in your readings, have a strong personal meaning for you.

Learning to Interpret New Stones

When you bring home a new stone, wash it carefully in mild soap and water and dry it off with a soft cloth. Don't put it in with the other stones until you've taken time to examine it and determine its interpretation. Just like the stones included with *The Crystal Tree*, any new stone you add will have three layers of meaning and a Shadow. Remember also that each stone has its place in the Tree of Life; new stones cannot be rightly interpreted until you've discovered where they fit into the Tree's structure.

The process of interpretation is not an inventive process; you are not making up a stone's meanings. Instead you are seeing it clearly and seeing beyond it to its connections with the Universe. As a created being, every stone has its place in the vast dance of creation. All things are alive in the sight of their maker; you are going to try to see this stone as alive, discover its meanings and connections.

To discover where each stone fits, take your time. Your goal is to reach a state of physical, emotional, and spiritual ease in which you feel ful energy. Relax yourself completely: yoga stretches may help, or reverently preparing and drinking a small pot of herbal tea. Whatever you do, do it thoroughly, easily, with no attitude of haste. If you do yoga, you know the techniques; if you opt for herbal tea, make it in a fine pot and drink it from a pretty cup. (Mint is very relaxing.) Shortcuts such as teabags and microwaves have no place here. The process is all-important.

When you are free of tension, take up the first stone and look at it. The following questions are designed to help you see in a way you ordinarily don't. For some people, the questions them-selves may become a ritual that helps you attain the necessary spiri-tual peace. Others will discard the questions when the stone itself takes over. Once you have gone through the interpretation with a stone, it's useful to check the questions again. You may find that in your reverent seeing you forgot to note touch impressions, or while lost in texture you missed variations of color.

What is the stone's color?

Does it have more than one color? How are they blended? Are there abrupt changes of color, or do they shade into one another? Visualize the stone's color as part of an embroidered hanging or a comfortable garment. What shapes does it take? Is there a taste, a touch, a sound, an emotion that you connect with the color?

What does the shape feel like?

Is the stone globular, oval, triangular, square, or does it have sev-eral shapes? Do the stone's changes in shape correspond with or contrast with changes in color and texture? Are there depressions in the rock? Does it fit only one way in the hand, or can it be turned over and over? What does the shape remind you of? Did it appear in your color meditations — and what color was it associated with? Freely imagine all sorts of other things that have the same general shape as the stone. Hold the stone in your hand: what does it want you to do?

What is the texture like?

Is the stone edged, rough, grainy, smooth, glassy? Is it all one tex-ture, or does the texture vary? Is it pitted? Does the stone stay cool in your hand or does it attract and hold warmth? Rub it against your palm, fingertips, lips, forehead. Imagine that texture against all your skin, surrounding you as water surrounds a swimmer. How does it make you feel?

Are there unusual features of this particular stone?

Look for fossils, for the line between matrix and crystal, for patterns in the stone. These features will influence the stone's interpretation. I have a lovely stone, half quartz and half citrine, that symbolizes transformations from flesh to spirit.

Where does it fit on the Tree of Life?

Visualize the stone in each of the ten sephiroth. How well does it seem to fit? Does it agree or quarrel with the sephiroth? Where would it be most powerful, where would it be blocked and unable to work? Could it fit in two or more sephiroth?

Find out what it's made of.

Stones you buy should be labelled. A field guide to stones and minerals will help you identify any stones you find. Then you can look up the materials that compose the stone — whether it's made of silicon or iron or sulphur. Think about the elements in the stone and about other things they are a part of.

How was the stone created?

Find out if the stone is igneous, metamorphic, or sedimentary. Igneous rocks, created in fire, tend to carry the meanings of fire (see the section on the four elements in chapter 6). Metamorphic rocks began as igneous or sedimentary rocks and were transformed by heat or pressure, usually becoming stronger and more coherent: this process will be reflected in the stone's meaning. Sedimentary rocks developed slowly and still reflect, in their layering and their many fossils, the conditions that prevailed when they were created; they are slow, steady, and conservative.

Thinking about the specific processes that shaped the stone can help you find keys to its nature. Pumice, for example, is lava that cooled very quickly — so quickly that it still has air bubbles in it. In texture, color, and meaning it suggests anger that rises quickly, scalds, and cools: it often shows up for the hasty, hot-tempered person who doesn't understand why the hurtful things he or she says while in a fury are taken to heart by others. Crystals are formed very slowly, deep underground. Like insight, they take time to grow and evolve. Generally, the more structured a rock is, the more slowly it was formed.

When you've handled the stone and examined it, relax and let images come to you. When you feel you've got the primary meaning of the stone, try to see how it works on all three levels. Then daydream a little and see the stone's Shadow. Write down the meanings the stone suggests and study them. Remember that the stones, as you get to know them better, will continue to reveal new meanings. As you become more aware, you will see more.

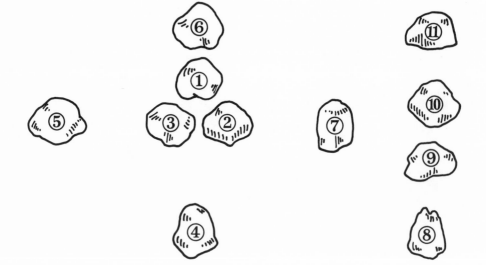

Figure 10.1 The Celtic Cross

10

Adding New Spreads

The Tree of Life is the basic structure on which *The Crystal Tree* is patterned. With its levels of meaning and its correspondences, the Tree of Life spread is the most comprehensive spread. But sometimes other spreads can be useful. If you want to chronologically trace the changes of a specific situation and see where it's headed, the Celtic Cross, for instance, is better. If you want to compare a horoscope with *The Crystal Tree*, the Twelve Houses spread is a good choice. As you become more attuned with the stones, other spreads — based on tarot, numerology, even palmistry — may suggest themselves to you.

The Celtic Cross

The Celtic Cross (see Figure 10.1) is familiar to almost anyone who has had a tarot reading: it is a very common spread for tarot cards. It is most useful in exploring a specific question about daily life, because it gives a focused, structured answer and a clear conclusion — even when the conclusion is to wait for further developments.

Lay out the stones on a flat surface, as usual, and don't begin to interpret until all the stones are selected and laid out. Before you begin interpreting, take a moment to study patterns of color, form, and clarity in the spread, just as you would with the basic Tree of Life spread.

The first stone represents the querent — the person asking the question — and symbolizes his or her place in the situation. Many card readers select a particular card for the querent, based on age, sex, and either physical appearance or Sun-sign element; I personally disagree with this practice, especially in connection with *The Crystal Tree*, and not only because there are no stones indicating coloring, age, or sex. When the stones are allowed to reveal which role the querent is playing, self-deception and stereotypes (of age, sex, and appearance) can't get in the way of genuine insight.

The "querent stone" may surprise you; sometimes a passive person will have an aggressive first stone, or a decisive person will have a confused and cloudy stone. Remember that people play different roles in different situations. If you're reading for yourself and feel the stone is inaccurate or surprising, you may want to decide which stone does seem to symbolize you and ponder the differences between the stones before going on with the interpretation.

The second stone "covers" the first — literally with cards, metaphorically with the stones. (Lay this stone to the lower right of the first stone; please don't lay it on top.) It symbolizes the atmosphere around the querent and any forces helping him or her.

The third stone "crosses" the first and second. Lay this stone to the lower left of the first stone, so that it forms a triangle with the other two; again, please don't lay it on top. This stone symbolizes antagonistic forces, problems or people to be struggled against, and very often the querent's private doubts and reservations about the question.

The fourth stone is laid below the triangle of the first three stones. This stone is the foundation stone; it reveals what lies at the bottom of the question — again, often a surprising stone, because the apparent or immediate cause of a situation is rarely the real root of it.

The fifth stone, laid to the left of the triangle, represents influences or events in the recent past that are just passing off. This stone may be the key to a successful conclusion. It indicates which feelings, forces, and ideas have less power or significance than they once did, and thus effectively reveals which way a situation is going. Because the influences symbolized here are weakening, they may show where the fortress can be breached or whether action is necessary at all. (Beware, though; if the influences symbolized here are of long standing, they will fight fiercely when attacked; "passing off" does not mean dead and gone!) If the influences were favorable to the querent's purpose, this stone shows where work is needed or perhaps which strategies have failed.

The sixth stone, laid at the top of the triangle, signifies the best results that can be achieved under current circumstances. Whether this stone is favorable or unfavorable, remember that situations change constantly. This stone is not the ultimate conclusion or even the short-term conclusion; it's the best the querent can do now.

The seventh stone, laid to the right of the triangle and completing the cross, continues the fifth stone's sense of movement. It indicates which way the situation will be moving in the near future.

The next four stones are laid in a vertical line — like a ladder — to the right of the basic triangle-cross figure. Again like a ladder, the first step is taken at the bottom. The eighth stone represents the querent's hopes in the situation. The ninth signifies the attitudes of family and friends. The tenth represents the querent's fears — and here you should stop. There is always a strong connection between the eighth and tenth stones; hopes balance and reflect fears, for they are the two poles of one situation. Spend whatever time is necessary to find the connection between them, for this is the principle on which the querent's attitude turns. The eleventh stone, the last, is placed at the top, and it reveals the resolution of the situation — not necessarily the final resolution, but how it will stand in the next six to twelve weeks.

If the reading has ended on a confused or unresolved note,

you can take it one step further. Take the last stone in the reading and use it as the first stone of a new Celtic Cross. (This bridge ensures continuity between the two readings.) Return the other stones to the bag and start again. The positions mean the same things each time you go through the Celtic Cross. The second reading, however, is usually less specific and accurate than the first, because many factors can change the situation before it occurs, including the reading and the querent's response to it.

The Twelve Houses

If you're familiar with astrology, you already know about the twelve houses of the horoscope. Each house deals with a different area of life; each has a natural ruler — the sign that naturally corresponds with the house and that sign's ruling planet. Once you've mastered the meanings of the twelve houses, you have another way to lay out the stones.

The houses are arranged in a circle like the face of a clock. The first house is at the place in the circle corresponding to 9 o'clock; the second at 8 o'clock, the third at 7 o'clock, and so on counterclockwise around the circle. (See Figure 10.2.) You can draw the circle yourself or, better still, find a blank horoscope form and use that to spread the stones on. Perhaps the best way is to use the querent's own horoscope chart to lay out the stones; analyzing and discussing correspondences between the stones and the houses of the querent's horoscope will greatly enrich the reading.

This reading is useful for character study by comparing the stones and the horoscope; for predicting long-term changes in self-image, values, and life situation; and for determining emotional compatibility by comparing the stones of the querent with the lover's horoscope chart. You can also ask a specific question and get a very detailed reading of its influence on every part of your life.

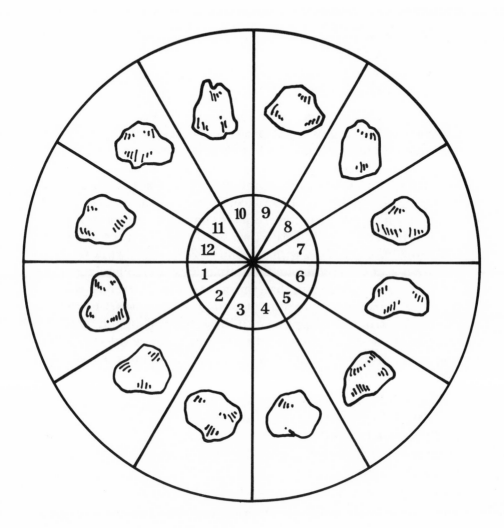

Figure 10.2 The Twelve Houses

The First House
Natural Ruler: Aries
Planet: Mars
Element: Fire

When you ask a specific question, the first house stone reveals which attitudes are most appropriate for success and whether your own natural approach is useful or destructive.

The first house represents the self in its pure form, unaware of anything but itself and its own needs. Before any learning, any nurturing, any civilizing takes place, there is still a character. The first house is the mirror that reflects character, the central core of the self. What quality best expresses the self? It's not what the self desires; that changes with age and circumstance. How the self gets what it desires is the one thing that doesn't change. Here the means are more important than the ends; even if the self is seeking true love, spiritual enlightenment, and peace on earth, the results can be disastrous if its approach to these is arrogant and destructive or mere wishful thinking. The first house, being ruled by Mars and Aries, deals with beginnings and aggression: how the self approaches (or attacks) life.

The Second House
Natural Ruler: Taurus
Planet: Venus
Element: Earth

When you ask a specific question, the second house stone reveals what you want from a given situation and what you are willing to give for it. The second house also signifies subconscious drives and desires.

The second house deals with having, in every sense of the word. Physical possessions come most easily to mind, but this house also deals with having convictions and values, "to have and to hold" or possessing another person in marriage, having (not just bearing or rearing) children. Having in the second house is the natural step beyond Getting in the first house; the second house cherishes, protects, keeps, and maintains.

Though in the first house the means were more important than the ends, in the second house the object — what is possessed — matters most. Why? Because the having itself tends to be the same. Whether caring for a lover or for wealth and position, the second house is blind to the object's faults, violent in its defense, obsessed with its welfare, and willing to sacrifice everything for the sake of the object. For the second house, where its treasure is, there is its heart also. The second house recognizes its object as being immeasurably superior (God, an ideal, a country) or helplessly inferior (a child, for example — even a grown-up child). Even the second-house love for a mate (only part of one's love for one's mate) is unequal, based not on realistic estimates of his or her character and capabilities, but simultaneously kneeling in adoration and hovering with protective fear.

The Third House
Natural Ruler: Gemini
Planet: Mercury
Element: Air

When you ask a specific question, the third house stone symbolizes communication and possible problems with communication. It also symbolizes friends who may help or hurt you in your endeavor.

The third house moves us into equality. The first house symbolizes pure self, knowing only its own drives and desires. The second house lavishes love, care, and attention on an object that is not an equal — sometimes not even a person. The third house is rational; it rules communication and social life. It is also the first reciprocal house; the first house acknowledges no other, and second-house love continues whether the love object returns love or not.

But communication is as much listening as talking; the third house recognizes not only that there are others but that they are equals with ideas and opinions of their own. Agreement and disagreement, truth and lies, like and dislike, all begin to have meaning; it's no wonder that this house traditionally handles duality and twinship! A new kind of love is possible in the third house, one based on more than primitive need or primitive protective instincts — based on friendship, equality, conversation. For the first time, presenting oneself well becomes important; thus both lies and fashion are associated with the third house.

The Fourth House
Natural Ruler: Cancer
Planet: The Moon
Element: Water

When you ask a specific question, the fourth house stone symbolizes the foundations and structures of the situation, the influence of your home and family, as well as balances and imbalances within the situation.

The fourth house takes us home. After the third house has recognized and communicated with others, the fourth house can create families and homes. Fourth house symbolism is usually of home and mother, of protective and nurturing care (but on a more ordinary, mundane basis than the almost idolatrous love of the second house), of affection and the small, ordinary trials of affection.

A strong fourth house gives courage and confidence; a weak one can contribute to insecurity, low self-esteem, and constant emotional ups and downs. This house is the foundation of all that follows; the stability of the number four is implicit in all it influences. Think of the things that come in fours: four seasons, four elements, four suits of the tarot, four compass directions, four levels of human existence (body, mind, soul, and spirit), four walls to build a basic house. Four suggests completion, natural stability, a kinship with the rhythms of the Universe: all the things a strong fourth house offers.

   With all the emphasis on stability and security here, one might argue that the Moon, which rules the fourth house, is inappropriate as this house's ruler. What is more inconstant than the Moon, never the same two nights in a row? Yet the Moon is constant; though it changes, it changes in a dependable way, and it maintains its orderly internal rhythms. Stability is not rigidity; it is the ability to adapt to constantly shifting circumstances without losing one's own integrity. Like a building made earthquake-proof, emotional foundations need to be a little flexible, to have just the right amount of give in them. That is the goal of wise nurturing: it provides the ability to stand on one's own. Unlike the second house, the fourth house knows that the child — or the lover, the idea, the friend, the self — needs room and independence to grow just as much as it needs love and care. Problems in the fourth house come when the rhythm is disturbed by too much distance or too little; too much protective care or not enough. Either extreme results in instability and self-doubt.

The Fifth House
Natural Ruler: Leo
Planet: The Sun
Element: Fire

When you ask a specific question, the fifth house stone symbolizes the self in the situation, self-image and self-doubt, and creativity, including creative or unusual solutions to problems.

   The fifth house relates back to the self again, but it has moved far beyond the self as it was in the first house — solely concerned with filling its needs, demonstrating individuality only by how it gets what it wants. The fifth house is built on the fourth house foundation of nurturing and freedom. It signifies the self in full glory, independent, proud, magnanimous. It's generosity comes more from overflowing spirits than from real sympathy, which requires identification with the sufferer — something the fifth house does not know how to do. Though it knows that others exist, it has yet to learn that they are selves too. Because creation is the ultimate expression of the self, the fifth house also deals with creativity in every form — painting, sculpting, keeping a journal, dreaming and daydreaming, dancing, crafts, gardening, whatever expresses the self.

The Sixth House
Natural Ruler: Virgo
Planet: Mercury
Element: Earth

When you ask a specific question, the sixth house stone symbolizes service to others, craftsmanship and your attitude toward work, and your search for perfection.

The sixth house rules service to others, health, self-sacrifice, a kind of sublimation of the instinctive, passionate protection of the second house. The sixth house is wise in the ways of giving and is less likely than the second house to smother the object. However, in its quest for perfection, the sixth house has gained a reputation for nagging, pettiness, and hypochondria.

How does one move from the shining glory of the fifth house to the practical goodness (or pickiness) of the sixth house?

The fifth house is a butterfly, so taken with its own bright wings that it tends to forget others. The sixth house is a bee, flying sturdily in the service of the whole hive. The difference between the fifth house and the sixth house is that the sixth house has learned to empathize with others in their suffering. The sixth house retains the fifth house's attitude of the splendor of the individual, but extends it to all individuals. Feeling that, what can the sixth house do but help those whose splendor has somehow been dimmed by fear, pain, or oppression? The notorious pickiness is a (perhaps misguided) attempt to bring perfection to everyone. The fifth house creativity also needs the sharp editorial eye and rigorous craftmanship of the sixth house if it is to become anything more than a hobby.

The Seventh House
Natural Ruler: Libra
Planet: Venus
Element: Air

When you ask a specific question, the seventh house stone symbolizes love, partnership, and marriage. Careful interpretation of the stones is necessary to separate wishful thinking from reality.

The seventh house, like all air houses, deals with communication, but this house moves beyond friendship and equality to the responsibilities and pleasures of committed love. In the seventh house, the sixth house practical concern for others is concentrated to a recognition of the need for fairness and justice. The seventh house is less likely to feed the poor than to educate them so they can feed themselves.

Personal relationships head the list of areas needing attention, partly because the seventh house realizes that in this area, one person can make a difference, and partly because the seventh house is less interested in people than in persons. Seventh-house love is idealistic and perhaps a little abstract. When there is a genuine commitment to the other person, seventh-house love can become extraordinarily strong, but it is untested; this house can drift away to fantasy love and sometimes lacks the energy to fight to save a relationship.

The Eighth House
Natural Ruler: Scorpio
Planet: Pluto
Element: Water

When you ask a specific question, the eighth house symbolizes endings, secrets, fears, and sexuality.

Like the fourth house, the eighth house deals with foundations, but it does not create them; it tests them. The dreamy love and untested commitment of the seventh house confront death

and sex in the eighth house and emerge utterly transformed —
if they survive the battle.

The eighth house has a difficult reputation. Sexuality and
death so often are treated sensationally that even their honest
manifestations seem frightening or taboo. The fourth house was
in tune with the universal rhythms of the seasons, the waxing and
waning moon, and the tides; the eighth house makes those
rhythms personal. Reproduction — sex — is made necessary by
death. Sexuality and child-bearing are thus intimately linked with
death: not just death in the abstract, but the death of the self. In
confronting the first, the self must admit to the inevitability of the
second. At that point regeneration begins. There is no death without resurrection; by the way the self lives, it chooses its own resurrection.

But death in the eighth house is more than physical death.
It is the ending of one kind of life and the beginning of another,
and it is both painful and necessary to growth. We shed our skins,
thinking them to be ourselves, and grieve as though we had indeed
died. In our resurrections we rejoice, forgetting that other deaths
await us.

The Ninth House
Natural Ruler: Sagittarius
Planet: Jupiter
Element: Fire

When you ask a specific question, the ninth house stone symbolizes
religion and philosophy, travel, adventure, and higher education.

From the ashes of the eighth house a new self emerges: spiritual and animal, philosopher and wanderer. Like the first house
self that knew itself only by blind wanting, like the fifth house self
that knew its own glory through self-expression, the ninth house
self begins a new cycle of learning. It has learned desire, protective
love, equality, stability, creativity, service, romantic love, and
death; having seen death, it now wants to know something of the

afterlife. Religion, philosophy, travel, and higher education all become important, because the ninth house knows what lasts: not possessions but thoughts and ideas, the things of the spirit and the mind.

The ninth house, having tasted death, is willing to enjoy physical delights as well as philosophical ones. It may be tempted into the eat-drink-and-be-merry attitude, knowing already what it is like to die. But in general, the ninth house strives for balance of the mind and body. Publishing, a ninth-house activity, is the perfect example: abstract ideas and imaginary characters are made concrete and lasting in the form of books.

The Tenth House
Natural Ruler: Capricorn
Planet: Saturn
Element: Earth

When you ask a specific question, the tenth house stone symbolizes money and business matters, as well as government or political issues.

In the progression towards independence and detachment, the tenth house is the pinnacle for the earth houses. The second house is blindly possessive of other people, the sixth house dedicated to serving and helping others, but the tenth house rules, manages, disciplines, and leads others — sometimes on a grand scale.

This house, the midheaven on the horoscope, represents success in the world. Ninth house philosophy and ideas must be turned to good (and being of earth, practical) use. Matters of business and administration are dealt with here; money and position are important in that they are useful ways of leading others. The danger here is of losing touch with the real public good; what seems to be service to others can rapidly become self-serving and destructive.

In its role as disciplinarian, the tenth house can again become enamored of power or even of inflicting pain and can cause appalling damage in the name of doing good. But overall, the tenth house is happiest working long hours, seven days a week, for the sake of a cause, and its disciplinary function is directly related to success.

The Eleventh House
Natural Ruler: Aquarius
Planet: Uranus
Element: Air

When you ask a specific question, the eleventh house stone signifies friendships, philanthropy, and universal love and communication.

The eleventh house is involved with more than ruling and organizing others; it believes in spreading new ideas that will allow people to rule themselves. Its belief that the truth will set you free makes the eleventh house egalitarian, open-minded, and generally tolerant. Like all the air houses, the eleventh house is intellectual and communicative. It has followed a logical cycle of development that began with the third house's discovery of equality and communication through the seventh house's discovery of romantic love to its own discovery of universal love. Though that universal love has traditionally been interpreted as friendship, friendship is only one manifestation of eleventh house energy.

The eleventh house works for freedom, usually by spreading a particular philosophy that it believes is the truth — any philosophy from Confucianism to democracy, from the need for universal medical care to the need for education in psychic work. The eleventh house's desire for the truth may break down here, and with it the desire for universal freedom: The philosophy or creed can become the goal, not the means to a goal, and at that point the eleventh house can become as intolerant and rigid as the ideas it's trying to displace.

The Twelfth House
Natural Ruler: Pisces
Planet: Neptune
Element: Water

When you ask a specific question, the twelfth house stone symbolizes the mystical impulse, religious feeling, and karmic debts that must be worked out.

The twelfth house brings eleventh house ideas back into the personal range. Instead of seeking freedom for the masses, as does the eleventh house, the twelfth house seeks personal holiness through mysticism, knowing that the world can be changed by prayer as well as by proselytizing. Like all the water houses, the twelfth house is concerned with the rhythms of the Universe and the progress of the soul. In the first of the water houses, the fourth house, foundations were built in accordance with the predictable changes of the Moon. In the eighth house, these foundations were tested by the twin fires of sex and death, which make the universal rhythms personal. In the twelfth, a temple is built in which it can become as one with the Universe.

In the twelfth house the concepts of personal and universal merge; the individual ideally becomes part of the cosmic dance, knowing that true freedom is doing the will of God. Inherent in the ecstacies of this merging with the all lie the risks: the twelfth house may love that sense of merging so much that it chooses the wrong things to merge with, being unable at the end to distinguish between God and other ecstatic experiences — drugs, sex, totalitarian mass movements, destructive relationships.

The twelfth house has been traditionally associated with karma, fate, self-undoing, and psychological repression. Its unpleasant reputation stems partly from misunderstanding of certain mystical disciplines and the idea of surrendering totally to God — which is really the intended end of every human soul — and partly from the problems a misdirected twelfth house can generate.

Appendix A

Summary of Instructions

To do a reading with *The Crystal Tree*, spread the Tree of Life board on a flat surface. Open the bag containing the stones. Close your eyes and meditate or concentrate on a specific question, person, or idea. Yes-or-no questions are not as good as open-ended questions. For example, instead of asking, "Should I change my job?", concentrate on "career." Reach into the bag, choose a stone, and place it on the Tree of Life board. The first stone drawn should be placed on the first circle (*sephirah*, plural *sephiroth*), the second stone on the second sephirah, and so on until ten stones have been drawn and each sephirah has been filled.

How do you choose a stone? It will simply feel right in your hand. Each stone has a characteristic vibration, which your own psychic abilities can sense. If you look at the stones while you choose, your conscious mind will take over (especially once you know the meanings of the stones) and you'll find yourself controlling the outcome. It's better to relax and trust your psychic sense. To prevent peeking, you may want to make a cloth bag to hold the stones.

Once the stones are laid out, don't be too quick to look up their meanings. Look first at the whole spread. Are the colors of stones and sephiroth harmonious, or do they clash? Are there clusters of one color? Which colors are missing in the spread? Look for patterns of color and shape. Do the stones fall in their natural places — that is, on the sephiroth with which they are naturally aligned — or are there conflicting aspects? Which stones are missing? Often what is missing is what's most significant. When you have truly grasped the whole, examine each part.

Starting at the top, with Crown, the first sephirah, look at each stone. Hold the stone you've placed on Crown in your hand and try to feel what it says to you. Does the color or shape remind you of anything? Is it pleasant or unpleasant to the eye and hand? Feel the edges and the weight; daydream a little, letting images flow into your mind. This is an important step in interpretation. Those images will provide the flow of psychic energy that links one stone with another and makes a reading significant.

Move next to the second sephirah, Wisdom, and repeat this process with the stone you've placed on it. Continue through the entire Tree, letting each of the stones "talk" to you before you look up their meanings. When you have sensed each stone — especially as you become more familiar with *The Crystal Tree* and the psychic flow — you may not need to look up the meanings. Brief interpretations of the stones are included below; longer, fuller ones will be found in chapter 2. Remember that the interpretation of a stone is greatly influenced by the sephirah where it is placed. Consult the brief list of the Sephiroth and their areas of influence (below); the longer section on their meanings is found in chapter 4.

There are three levels of meaning listed for every stone. The physical level deals with daily events and ordinary life. The psychological level is more concerned with motivations and personal growth. The spiritual level deals with the progress of the soul. (*The Crystal Tree* is non-denominational; it can be used for purely secular purposes as well as for serious spiritual insight, depending on what the user wants.)

Then there is the Shadow. The Shadow is the negative side of every positive quality, and it should be taken into account, along with the more pleasant side of every interpretation. The Shadow is always there; it's up to you whether to emphasize it or concentrate on the positive side. You won't get rid of the Shadow by ignoring it or repressing it, but by knowing it exists and guarding against it.

The full interpretations in the text and the capsule interpretations here will help you to understand your readings, but don't rely on them too much. Stones are individualists, and you may find that one stone or another has taken on new meaning to you.

How to Identify the Stones

Red

Rose quartz: translucent, pale pink
Red cullet: transparent, blood red

Orange

Jasper: opaque, dark orange, fine-grained
Carnelian: semi-opaque, orange, no grain, often banded

Brown/Yellow

Cat's-eye: opaque, yellowish brown, shines like satin
Brown agate: translucent brown, sometimes banded with white

Green

Green quartz: opaque, mottled pale green
Aventurine: opaque, shiny, dark green

Blue/Grey

Hematite: opaque, metallic steely gray
Sodalite: opaque, very dark blue

Purple

Chevron amethyst: translucent, purple banded with clear or white
Amethyst: translucent, rich purple

White/Clear

Crystal (clear): clear as glass
Crystal (half-clear): cloudy
Silent stone: opaque, white

Black/Grey

Montana agate: cloudy, translucent, with dark flecks
Smoky quartz: dark grey, translucent when held to light
Onyx: opaque, black, shiny

A Brief Interpretation of the Stones

Rose Quartz
Sephirah: Crown

Physical: Friendship, intimacy, closeness.
Psychological: Harmony and affection; close family ties; the need for love and approval.
Spiritual: Surrender to God.
Shadow: Giving in, lack of self-assertion, going along with the crowd.

Red Cullet
Sephirah: Crown

Physical: Individualism, passion, and sexuality.
Psychological: Passion, creation, art. Independence and rebellion.
Spiritual: Spiritual transformation and renewal, the spirit of seeking.
Shadow: Jealousy, self-centeredness.

Jasper
Sephirah: Wisdom

> **Physical:** Restlessness, change, curiosity.
> **Psychological:** Spirit of seeking, self-examination, analysis.
> **Spiritual:** The spirit of the quest, of the pilgrim.
> **Shadow:** Change for its own sake — or the refusal to change

and grow.

Carnelian
Sephirah: Understanding

> **Physical:** Warm and affectionate friendships, parties, and cele-

brations.

> **Psychological:** Emotional ties based on knowledge of the other
> person, not on mystery and uncertainty. The need to understand and
> analyze relationships.
> **Spiritual:** Reverence for life. The attitude that pleasure is of God
> and is therefore holy. Mystical union with God and all creation.
> **Shadow:** Manipulativeness, lack of self-respect, overindulgence,

hiding behind a social group.

Cat's-Eye
Sephirah: Mercy

> **Physical:** Insight, shrewdness, vision.
> **Psychological:** The gift of understanding others' problems. Often
> the mark of someone who is dedicated to helping others.
> **Spiritual:** Willingness to forgive, understanding the flaws of your-
> self and others.
> **Shadow:** Judgmental spirit, catiness, gossip.

Brown Agate
Sephirah: Severity

> **Physical:** Caution and good judgment. Slow and careful prep-

aration.

Psychological: Self-discipline.
Spiritual: Penance, justice, scrupulous fairness.
Shadow: Pessimism, gloom, worry, often over petty matters. Insecurity and fear.

Green Quartz
Sephirah: Beauty

Physical: Strength of character, self-esteem.
Psychological: Blending the unconscious with the conscious. Willingness to face your own dark side. The ability to interpret dreams.
Spiritual: The Kingdom of God within you.
Shadow: Nightmares, phobias, emotional problems. The separation of spiritual and physical life.

Aventurine
Sephirah: Beauty

Physical: Great physical enjoyment, health, taking pleasure in the body.
Psychological: Balance between body, soul, and spirit. A healthy and innocent enjoyment of physical pleasures.
Spiritual: Freely offering of the body to God.
Shadow: Physical illness, stress, and separation from (or too much absorption in) the body.

Hematite
Sephirah: Victory

Physical: Enduring love, desire controlled by idealism, complete commitment.
Psychological: The discipline to transform dreams into reality. Sustained commitment to a dream.
Spiritual: Continuing devotion to God despite adverse circumstances.
Shadow: Rigidity, fault-finding. Inability to make a commitment or stick to a project.

Sodalite
Sephirah: Splendor

Physical: Achievement, success, hard work rewarded.
Psychological: Getting your just deserts — knowing what you deserve and asking for it.
Spiritual: Freedom from greed, taking no thought for the morrow.
Shadow: Materialism, greed, lack of compassion.

Chevron Amethyst
Sephirah: Foundation

Physical: Organization, structure, neatness.
Psychological: The final integration of the personality.
Spiritual: The order of heaven.
Shadow: Snobbishness, wrong priorities, inhuman bureaucracy.

Amethyst
Sephirah: Kingdom

Physical: Psychic talents combined with common sense. Great success.
Psychological: Psychic powers used well, self-knowledge and self-control.
Spiritual: A true spirit. Proper values.
Shadow: Using psychic knowledge for destructive purposes (very dangerous).

Crystal (clear)

Physical: Psychic abilities and clarity of outlook. Emotional harmony and peace.
Psychological: The integrated personality. Good relationships with others based on self-respect.
Spiritual: Clear views of spiritual truth.
Shadow: Arrogance, fear of change.

Crystal (half-clear)

Physical: Confusion, hasty or prejudiced thinking. Not letting yourself see the whole situation.

Psychological: Hiding the truth from yourself (usually to protect someone else).

Spiritual: The beginning of wisdom: knowing that you don't know.

Shadow: Refusing to trust yourself.

Silent stone (white)

Physical: New beginnings and ideas.

Psychological: Waiting for the right time to make new beginnings.

Spiritual: The start of a new way of thinking. Protecting new ideas from hostile people.

Shadow: Overcaution or overeagerness.

Montana Agate

Physical: Memories and persons from the past turn up. Opportunities to correct past mistakes.

Psychological: Unconscious worries or influences from the past.

Spiritual: Remembering past problems in order to avoid them in the future.

Shadow: Restraint, fear, lack of forgiveness of yourself and others.

Smoky Quartz

Physical: The ability or need to conceal yourself from other people. A dramatic temperament.

Psychological: Hiding your true self in order to be liked or accepted. Adaptability.

Spiritual: Struggling to find a true path. The faith is there, but the way is not evident.

Shadow: Self-blame, oversensitiveness.

Onyx

Physical: Strength, courage, endurance.

Psychological: Getting to the root of the problem — a painful but necessary process.

Spiritual: Rebirth after a period of suffering and dryness.

Shadow: Giving up; refusing to enjoy anything for fear it will be taken away.

A Guide to the Sephiroth

Crown

In Hebrew, Kether. Crown symbolizes pure energy, the self, individuality, growth, ambition.

Wisdom

In Hebrew, Chokmah. Wisdom represents instinctive knowing, the dark side, the unconscious, balance and imbalance, the object of a search, motives.

Understanding

In Hebrew, Binah. Understanding relates to primary emotional ties, relations with family and friends, social life.

Mercy

In Hebrew, Chesed. Mercy (also translated as Grace) signifies hope, areas of comfort and solidity, gifts and strengths, positive qualities.

Severity

In Hebrew, Din or Geburah. Severity (also translated as Judgment) indicates fears, areas of struggle and risk, drawbacks, restraints, problems.

Beauty

In Hebrew, Tiphareth. Beauty symbolizes balance, harmony, creative energy, health, the physical body.

Victory

In Hebrew, Netzach. Victory relates to discipline and desire, limits and drives, romantic love, commitment, the intellect, art, and creativity.

Splendor

In Hebrew, Hod. Splendor signifies rewards and results, work, money, children, craftsmanship.

Foundation

In Hebrew, Yesod. Foundation represents the structure of the soul, spiritual life and relationships, psychic work.

Kingdom

In Hebrew, Malkkuth. Kingdom is associated with the physical Universe, the shape of a life, the ultimate outcome of a problem, earthly success.

Appendix B

Recording Your Readings

Astrological Tree of Life for _____

Birthdate _____   Ascendant _____

Sun _____   Moon _____

Mercury _____   Venus _____

Mars _____   Jupiter _____

Saturn _____   Uranus _____

Neptune _____   Pluto _____

The Astrological Tree of Life

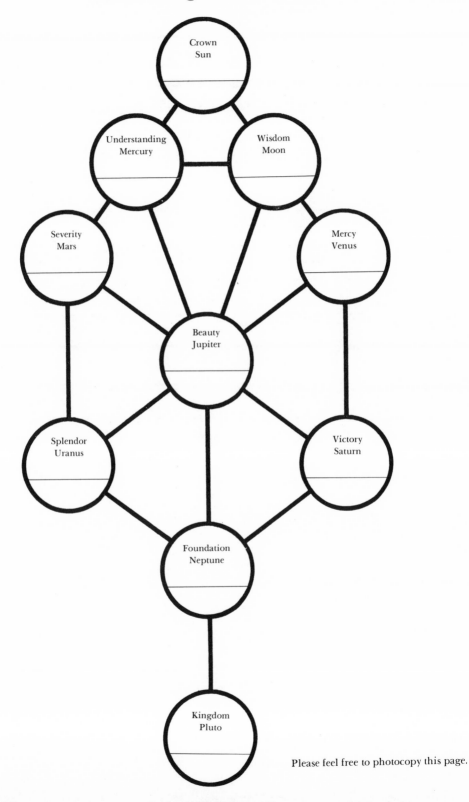

Crown
Sun

Understanding
Mercury

Wisdom
Moon

Severity
Mars

Mercy
Venus

Beauty
Jupiter

Splendor
Uranus

Victory
Saturn

Foundation
Neptune

Kingdom
Pluto

Please feel free to photocopy this page.

Reading for ______________________________

Day ____________________ Question ____________________

Interpretation ______________________________

____

____

____

____

____

____

____

Please feel free to photocopy this page.

Records of Your Readings

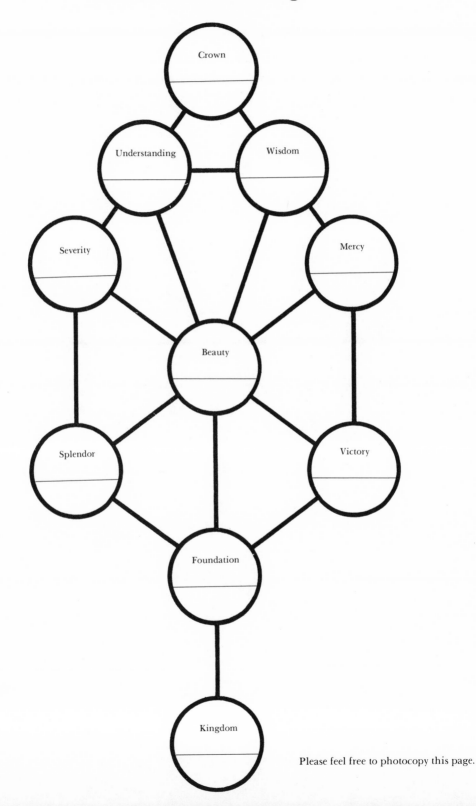

Please feel free to photocopy this page.

Further Reading

This bibliography is by no means a complete guide to books on the psychic arts; it does list those books I have found most helpful in explaining the principles behind them.

Astrology

Arroyo, Stephen. *Astrology, Psychology, and the Four Elements: An Energy Approach to Astrology & Its Use in the Counseling Arts.* Reno, NV: CRCS Publications, 1975.

Cunningham, Donna. *An Astrological Guide to Self-Awareness.* Reno, NV: CRCS Publications, 1978.

_____. *Being a Lunar Type in a Solar World.* York Beach, ME: Samuel Weiser, 1982.

Hand, Robert. *Horoscope Symbols.* Rockport, MA: Para Research, 1981.

Lundsted, Betty. *Astrological Insights into Personality.* San Diego, CA: Astro Computing Services, 1980.

Meyer, Michael R. *A Handbook for the Humanistic Astrologer.* Garden City, NY: Anchor Press/Doubleday, 1974.

Oken, Alan. *The Horoscope, The Road and Its Travelers: A Manual of Consciousness-Expanding through Astrology.* New York: Bantam Books, 1974.

Numerology

Campbell, Florence. *Your Days Are Numbered; A Manual of Numerology for Everybody.* Ferndale, PA: The Gateway, 1931.

Javane, Faith, and Dusty Bunker. *Numerology and the Divine Triangle.* Rockport, MA: Para Research, 1979.

Konraad, Sandor. *Numerology: Key to the Tarot.* Rockport, MA: Para Research, 1983.

Sepharial. *The Kabala of Numbers.* Van Nuys, CA: Newcastle, 1974.

Tarot

Blakeley, John D. *The Mystical Tower of the Tarot.* London: Robinson and Watkins, 1974.

Butler, Bill. *Dictionary of the Tarot.* New York: Schocken, 1975.

Douglas, Alfred. *The Tarot: The Origins, Meanings, and Uses of the Cards.* Harmondsworth, England: Penguin, 1972.

Jewels of the Wise. San Francisco: Epiphany Press, 1979.

Keystone of Tarot Symbols. San Francisco: Epiphany Press, 1979.

Laurence, Theodor. *How the Tarot Speaks to Modern Man.* Harrisburg, PA: Stackpole Books, 1972.

Nichols, Sallie. *Jung and Tarot: An Archetypal Journey.* York Beach, ME: Samuel Weiser, 1980.

Walker, Barbara G. *The Secrets of the Tarot: Origins, History, and Symbolism.* New York: Harper and Row, 1984.

General

Cavendish, Richard. *The Black Arts.* New York: Putnam, 1967.

_____. *Man, Myth, and Magic: An Illustrated Encyclopedia of the Supernatural.* New York: Marshall Cavendish, 1970.

Cooper, J.C. *An Illustrated Encyclopaedia of Traditional Symbols.* London: Thames and Hudson, 1978.

Gibson, Walter B., and Litzka R. Gibson. *The Complete Illustrated Guide to the Psychic Sciences.* New York: Bantam, 1968.

Graves, Robert. *The White Goddess: A Historical Grammar of Poetic Myth.* 2d. edition. New York: Farrar, Straus and Giroux, 1966.

Harding, M. Esther. *Woman's Mysteries, Ancient and Modern: A Psychological Interpretation of the Feminine Principle as Portrayed in Myth, Story, and Dreams.* New York: Bantam, 1973.

Heline, Corinne. *Mysteries of the Holy Grail.* Los Angeles: New Age Press, 1977.

Jung, C. G. *Analytical Psychology: Its Theory and Practice.* New York: Vintage, 1968.

_____. *Psychological Types.* Translated by H.G. Baynes, revised by R.F.C. Hull. Princeton, NJ: Princeton University Press, 1971.

_____, ed. *Man and His Symbols.* New York: Dell, 1968.

Jung, Emma, and Marie-Louise von Franz. *The Grail Legend.* Translated by Andrea Dykes. Boston: Sigo Press, 1986.

LeShan, Lawrence. *The Medium, the Mystic, and the Physicist: Toward a General Theory of the Paranormal.* New York: Viking, 1966.

Schaya, Leo. *The Universal Meaning of the Kabbalah.* Translated by Nancy Pearson. Baltimore, MD: Penguin, 1973.

Walker, Barbara G. *The Woman's Encyclopedia of Myths and Secrets.* New York: Harper and Row, 1983.

Wilson, Colin. *Mysteries.* New York: Vintage, 1977.

_____. *The Occult: A History.* New York: Vintage, 1973.